Too Hot to Handle

Fiona Pitt-Kethley

Too Hot to Handle

Peter Owen • *London*

PETER OWEN PUBLISHERS
73 Kenway Road London SW5 0RE

First published in Great Britain 1992
© Fiona Pitt-Kethley 1992

*The endpapers are based on a painting of Mademoiselle Rosalie Duthé
(dancer and mistress of Louis XVI) by Antoine Vestier (1740–1824).
Private collection, Paris.*

A catalogue record for this book is
available from the British Library

ISBN 0–7206–0875–9

Printed in Great Britain by Billings of Worcester

Contents

Acknowledgements

Although none of the articles in this book were published by their original commissioners, some were subsequently printed in *Forum*, *Passport* and *Poetry Review*.

Killed Articles

Introduction

I sometimes think I started conservation. Long before every thinking person turned Green, I was a voice crying in the wilderness (or rather, Haberdashers' Aske's Girls' School). As a young child I saw the beauty and worth of plants that others discarded, and started my own weed sanctuary, saving and recording what I could. On the principle of everything having a purpose, I also believed in make do and mend. Old materials and old paper were put to new use. I carried this same attitude into the rest of my life. All experience is useful. Everything, even the bad, can be learned from and written about. This book is in a sense about salvaging waste – articles that were not allowed to reach the public, private letters to someone I once loved.

For the first year or so of my career as a journalist, I was lucky, my articles suffered only the most minor cuts and alterations. Sometimes these were amusing ones, as when some mischievous editor or printer at *The Independent* altered 'A Sicilian I had met' to 'A Sicilian I had'. I was in no position to complain or sue for libel as I *had* had him. Journalists, like prostitutes, do what they do principally for the money. At the same time, though, we yearn for fame, to get our names recognised or, at the very least, to be read. It's a truth little known outside the profession that having an article commissioned by an editor provides no guarantee whatsoever that it will be published. When working for a magazine or newspaper a freelance rarely deals with the man or woman at the top. Beneath that person there's a whole network of other editors. Some have the power to commission, others have the power to kill. You can flog your guts out researching a story, deliver it on time and beautifully written, only to find that X doesn't want the piece that Y commissioned, mainly because X never liked you or your writing in the first place. Sometimes the reasons for

9

killing a feature are more complex – censorship comes into it. I don't mean merely that they don't like four-letter words – that kind of bowdlerisation could easily be agreed beforehand. It's something much more sinister. Often there's an unspoken rule: a writer is simply not allowed to hold an opinion that differs materially from the line taken by the paper, nor is the writer allowed to attack establishment figures. I find stories are axed if I mention certain names, however verifiable my comments about them are.

Commissioning editors like to have a drawerful of accepted manuscripts so that they can look prepared for every occasion. They think little of wasting large amounts of money on buying too many articles for too little space. Decades ago, things were very different. My grandfather, Victor Pitt-Kethley, was editor of *The Wide World* for fifty years. He valued his employer's money as if it were his own. Throughout his long spell as editor he never killed an article – he just half-killed them with rewriting. In his case, the urge to reword everything was probably pardonable. Virtually none of the pieces used were by professional writers. The magazine purported to be one that contained only true stories of adventure. His contributors were, therefore, explorers first and writers second.

What does a professional writer feel when his/her piece is shelved indefinitely or killed? I can't speak for the others but, personally, it's a bit like being a stand-up comic whose jokes have all fallen flat, or a woman who's made a pass and been refused. I resent it. In the most flagrant cases I feel bitterness against those involved. Because I'm a published writer with a name, they knew my style before they hired me. I always deliver copy on or before time and conform to synopses, so why won't they print what I have to say? There's a kind of implication (usually, but not always, unspoken) that what I have done isn't up to their exacting standards. But look at the average newspaper – even a quality one – and what do you see? A newspaper is not a world classic. We are not talking about the works of Shakespeare, just your average edition of *The Independent*, *The Times*, *The Guardian*, *New Woman* or whatever. Look at any 'quality newspaper' and you'll find at least ten indifferently written articles in it. If you're lucky, there may be one original piece of writing that makes you think. Even then, what are the odds that you'll save that article, or even remember the name of its writer for more than a day or two? Journalism, by the very meaning of the word, is about today, not yesterday or tomorrow. Newspapers are ephemeral – today's mental fodder, tomorrow's fish and chip wrapper.

I managed to obtain payment for all the commissioned pieces included here except the pilot for *The Spectator* and three of the 'Ars Amatoria' columns. In the materialistic sense, at any rate, the time spent writing them was not wasted. My one essay at writing love letters proved less fruitful. My passion was only very slightly requited and, by any standards, I was badly treated by the man concerned. I have included a selection from several years' worth of this correspondence as the second part of this book, with a separate introduction and notes placing each letter in context.

Fiona Pitt-Kethley
1992

Notes on Articles

Flowers and Candlelit Dinners was commissioned by *New Woman*. Over two months after I'd delivered the piece I had heard nothing and so contacted the magazine. I was told they did not want it and was offered half the original fee. As no 'kill fee' had been agreed I was determined to exact the full amount. I tried to do this by letter but received no answer. By then about eleven weeks had passed since I had submitted the piece. Feeling it was probably the only way to secure my money, I decided to exact payment like a bailiff. I sneaked into *New Woman's* offices and asked to see the editor. I told her that I had come to collect my cheque and that I had food and books to sustain me even if it took a week. Half a Trollope novel and a muesli bar (four hours) later I got my cheque. I had figured I would. If they'd thrown me out forcibly, I'd have shown my bruises to the *Evening Standard* and told them I was owed money. If they'd left me there for the night I could have used their facilities to photocopy the *Encyclopaedia Britannica* and phone New York, not to mention doing unmentionable things in their waste-paper baskets.

A Cuckoo in the Nest was one of three short pilot pieces that I wrote for *The Spectator*. My agent had suggested me as a nature columnist to the editor, who specified that I must turn in three articles in the next two weeks. I felt at that stage that it would probably be a thankless (and unpaid) task. An editor who took me seriously would have asked for only one trial piece, I thought. Anything else was probably just nuisance value.

Blow Jobs was commissioned by Michael VerMeulen of *GQ* over a lavish Japanese lunch. I had warned him in a synopsis that I found the act a bit boring but, nothing deterred, he told me to go ahead and write the piece. In the event my article was turned down with a pre-arranged kill fee. (I had told Michael of my run-in with *New Woman* so I expect he was especially careful to have a written contract.) Other pieces we'd talked of my doing never materialised. A lecturer I met later, who knew the magazine's editors, claimed that they'd turned the article down because 'They were a bit miffed you weren't all that keen on fellation!' *Forum* (female editorship) was happy to print the piece in full at a later date.

The next two articles were commissioned by Andy Bull of *The Independent*. I had worked for the paper on a semi-regular basis for a year, with approximately one article a month being commissioned. **Macho Feminists** was accepted but laid aside for twelve months. **Advice to Young Poets** was commissioned but returned as if it were unsolicited by the magazine's 'Living' pages editor. Perhaps wrongly, I have always held her responsible for the end of my career with *The Independent*. She had had a year off for pregnancy, during which time her replacements had gladly used articles by me. Some women with young babies turn very righteous and want to clean up the world. This, in practice, means that they must force people like me out of work. I asked for payment for this article and found that the other one had been killed, even though I had rewritten it considerably to my editor's instructions. It was extremely difficult to get money from *The Independent* for **Advice to Young Poets**. It took so many months that I was strongly tempted to go and do my bailiff act in their offices in City Road. Of all the 'kills' in this book I feel most bitter about these ones, because they ended a friendly relationship in which I felt able to offer ideas to the paper. I haven't yet managed to establish a similar situation with another national newspaper.

Platonic Friendships was written for a men's magazine called *ISM* which never quite got off the ground.

Le Weekend was commissioned at two days' notice for the first number of *The Times*'s 'Weekend' section by Brigid Callaghan and has been shelved indefinitely even though I had to do massive rewrites. She swears that the second version is not 'killed' but merely 'sleeping'. I have chosen the better, earlier version here.

Some Like It Hot was commissioned by the *Daily Mail* at four hours' notice. I phoned it in in time but suddenly the heavens opened and the story was not thought appropriate once the heat wave had broken.

Standard Diary was commissioned by the *Evening Standard* for page 9 at a day's notice. I was never able to catch the relevant editor on the phone to find out what happened to it. Maybe he just didn't like tom cats, or thought my jokes about salmonella were in poor taste.

The next four pieces were all written for my monthly 'Ars Amatoria' column for *The Guardian*. **Poethons and Sex Talk** bit the dust owing to my editor being away on holiday. The next, **Pensioners and Poetry Editors**, was dropped due to my having come down too hard on war veterans and also due to a possibly libellous story about Craig Raine. In the interests of not getting sued I have removed that story in this version – the veterans can look after themselves! **Beastly Behaviour** was accepted by the Arts Editor but killed while she was away on holiday by the Features Editor on the grounds that it didn't have enough about the arts in it. **Something Borrowed, Something Blue** . . ., another 'Ars Amatoria' column, perhaps went down because I sent my editor two pieces simultaneously, thus offering choice. My 'Ars Amatoria' column has subsequently been killed altogether by the new Arts Editor.

Educating Nigel is a short dialogue that was commissioned by Max Stafford-Clark of the Royal Court. He commissioned a series of such pieces from various well-known writers to celebrate the opening of the Theatre Upstairs. More than could be performed were written. Mine was one of those that fell by the wayside.

Flowers and Candlelit Dinners

Florists will hate me, Berkertex may well send round a hit squad and I will probably be haunted by Barbara Cartland, but I have to say that none of the romantic trappings means a thing to me.

Just before Christmas I received my first ever long-stemmed rose, which came in a cardboard box from Guernsey. Inside, a pinched frost-bitten bud reclined in a plastic tube. The instructions told me to fill its little stand with water, turn the flower round and insert the end of the stem in the slit provided. The package was about as romantic as a furled umbrella. The flower has yet to open out or give any vestige of a rose-like smell. I much prefer the greenflyed versions that have bloomed surprisingly late in my garden this year.

David, the sender of the rose, is one of my fans. He started his whirlwind courtship several weeks back with a seventeen-page letter claiming he'd spent a night with me twenty years ago and that he'd like to renew the acquaintance by having sex with me 'without the Pill'. I would have to define David as a romantic because he believes that he is my Mr Right. (I have another fan in Jedda who is also convinced that he is my destined partner, which complicates things.) David has said categorically that he is the only man for me and he is firmly convinced that we will marry in six months' time. He also promises me a climax, not 'just an orgasm'. David and I have never met. He has read my books and I have seen a mugshot of him – one that was not a pretty sight even by machine standards – but that is where the relationship ends as far as I am concerned.

The one thing that David has in common with other romantics is a complete inability to see the situation as it is. He is forty-eight, poor and exceptionally illiterate but does not see any of these things as obstacles because he has this tremendous 'love' to offer me. Love is a very questionable offering. A lot of nasty things are done in its name. People die for it and kill for it.

As a general rule I have found that men who give flowers within relationships are old-fashioned and manipulative. I can think of various occasions where I was persuaded to hang on to some bore for a little longer because of a small gift. I'm not mercenary, but it would seem churlish to tell someone to piss off after the roses or the pot plant came. The givers know that it's a passport to another date, however critical and unpleasant they've been before. Next time I'm presented with some flowers I mean to have the courage to resist this sort of emotional black-mail.

Flowers are bad emblems for a relationship anyway. They wither all too soon. I sometimes wish that a man would have the character (and enough faith in my green fingers) to offer me a packet of seeds instead – perhaps some unusual herb or wild flower ones. Seeds have a wonderful growth potential. My garden is still coming up forget-me-nots from ten years ago. Then there was the 22p's worth of broccoli that increased and multiplied horribly until it put me off eating the stuff for life, and the red cabbages which were cross-pollinated with every-thing else by some geriatric bee until the whole garden turned purple. Seeds are fun because you can't visualise the full con-sequences in advance.

Romance is a purely commercial invention to prey on peo-ple's pockets. It's as surely a con as the old Find the Lady game. From long-stemmed roses and Valentines up to the complete wedding-day package, romance has made millions from suckers everywhere. Most of the women I know enjoy sex. Why should they need persuaders along the road to it, if they've taken up with someone they fancy? If you like a man's company he shouldn't have to bribe you with roses. If you don't fancy or like the man you're going out with then drop him fast. It's less cruel than hanging on in the long run. Staying with someone for the material things they can provide is the worst, most dishonest form of prostitution.

Some people might argue that romance isn't about giving gifts and spending money, it's about creating a mood. They must be rather undersexed to need all that, or not as keen on their partner as they're pretending to be. (Romance all comes down to dishonesty.) Take dinner by candlelight – what's nice about candlelight? Candles smell. A silver candlestick can be an artistic object, but it looks decidedly better by electric light. Of course, the soft light may be required to stop you seeing your lover properly. If you can't stand the sight of your beloved by daylight, then it's time to trade him or her in for a new model.

Meeting points are another, romantic issue. I remember suggesting a rendezvous with one man outside a busy modern station in Rome. Oh no, that wasn't a romantic enough place for him, he said. I went to meet him by his choice – a bridge – but the bugger never showed up. Give me reliability by a dustbin, any day.

Past experiences have taught me that romantics are to be avoided at all costs. They are always the falsest of people. I have had a lot of undying love sworn to me by men who just wanted a one-night stand. The romantics were always the quickest to get the hell out in the unfriendliest way. I was only interested in temporary affairs with them – luckily. If I'd believed all that drivel about 'being together for ever', etc. I'd be a very unhappy person now. Fortunately, Byron had it wrong and love can be 'a thing apart' in a woman's life too. Now that women have their own careers they do not need to rely on men. It's time for the old con element to be thrown out of relationships.

Romantic books fuel the stereotypes with their virgin brides marrying older experienced men. Romance and inequality always go hand in hand. The brides in these books marry in white with all the trimmings. That sort of wedding is probably the most obnoxious manifestation of the connection between romance and commerce. It has absolutely nothing to do with love. It's about trading chicken in a basket and cheap champagne for an electric toaster or a Teasmade. It's also about showing off. The idea is not only to keep up with the Joneses, but to make them positively green with envy. If they had a Mercedes you must have a white Rolls-Royce. Worst of all is the would-be aristocratic bride who rides round the town in a coach and four. Every time I see one of those I wish some horse with a sense of humour would tow the whole equipage off to a brewery and drown his sorrows in a pint of Webster's bitter.

Wedding clothes are essentially old-fashioned. Most of the outfits worn by brides, bridesmaids and guests are totally ludicrous. Those who never wear hats ordinarily feel they must at weddings. The grooms frequently look like drunken undertakers. Most women dress far better on the average night out than on the great day. The bride generally looks worst of all, for one simple reason – white doesn't suit the majority of people. When it's all over there are the permanent mementoes. Photo albums were bad enough, but now you can bore all your friends and relatives to death with a video of the great day.

Will I ever marry? Perhaps, if I can find someone I like as well as fancy. I don't think sexual attraction is enough to base a long relationship on. I've been attracted to many men but would have considered a life tied to any of them as an unmitigated disaster. I wouldn't have had a career if I'd opted for that.

What is my ideal type? Rochester's too old and Heathcliff's too rough. I once met a perfect man and wrote a poem about him. He gave flowers too, come to think of it. He was so perfect that he once complained I'd lowered the tone of our conversation. Save me from perfect men. I'd like a nice liberated one who doesn't even notice when I swear; one who tolerates my sense of humour even at its most bizarre. One who can cap my jokes with blacker ones. I once met a man like that and fell madly in love with him until I found out he wasn't interested in sex. You can't have everything, it seems. Ideally I am looking out for that man's mind reincarnated in a toy-boy's body with plenty of stamina; and if he gives me a packet of seeds, so much the better.

A Cuckoo in the Nest

There's an old joke about a female parrot who produced four eggs, out of which stepped a magpie, two crows and a budgie. The punchline of the joke was: 'That's not a parrot – it's a prostitute.' The joke may not, it seems, be so far from the truth. Though birds don't generally cross-breed, they certainly can't be said to cross their legs. I had always taken with a pinch of salt those poetic tales about birds pairing for life. How on earth does anyone tell one blackbird from another, anyway? The little brown bird could be having a stream of black lovers calling, for all most of us know. My cynical suspicions have been confirmed by recent research in America (where else?). Somebody has had the bright idea of doing paternity tests on fledglings and has found that 30 per cent of them aren't sired by the resident male in the nest. Birds, it seems, have the knack of separate fertilisation of eggs. Every egg can have a different dad – in theory.

However, it still seems that pairing for life is found among many species. The bit romantic naturalists hadn't worked out is that this is solely to aid in bringing up their young. Fidelity is not a part of the bargain. The average ornithological marriage is an open one with adultery galore and the odd gang bang on the side. I am beginning to understand why bird-watchers lie for hours in marshes staring through pairs of binoculars. I might even take it up myself.

Even swans and turtle-doves, it turns out, are as promiscuous as the sparrow, which is famed for its lechery. How many bird books, not to mention much of English literature, will have to be rewritten in the light of this new evidence? Farmers have always known that cockerels were Don Juans. The proverbial cock on the dunghill has frequently been known to die a glorious death while coping with a whole yard-full of hens, although I don't suppose there's any chance of this happening on a factory farm. Pigeons, also, are very obviously not saints. I found out about them at a tender age. My father rescued one that could not fly and it sat around in a box for months. In sunny weather we opened the window and its boyfriends came in to see it. We christened the fattest, most violent one Albert, because he had the look of a Victorian or Edwardian swell. He used to knock poor Lucy down, rape her, steal her food, then put on a display outside with the other, less handicapped females in his life. Letting children view nature in the raw can be very corrupting. Perhaps a tastefully edited porno film would have made me less cynical.

My next-door neighbour does his best to attract birds, although he hasn't yet got it right. He has the sort of garden people come from miles away to take pictures of, even though there's only a couple of yards of it. It's not the flowers, nice enough though they are – it's the constructions. He's made a sort of hand-crafted model village for birds, complete with captions: 'The Rest-a-while Cabin – free accommodation for young and old feathered birds', or 'The Sparrow Hotel – all meals free'. The whole thing reminds me of an American ghost town. It's always empty. About the only feathered friend that comes down there is a large herring gull who slithers off the roof and crash-lands amongst the empty hotels for a quick raid on the crumbs. Like some people I know, gulls seem to rate junk food as highly as sex. Song-birds, of course, are more ethereal in their tastes – albeit in an earthy sort of way. Perhaps a model red-light district, with nests to be rented by the day, would have proved a greater pull to your average sparrow.

Blow Jobs

The Romans called it *fellatio*. They had a verb which meant to suck cocks and another which meant to fuck someone's mouth. These words turn up frequently in the best classical Latin epigrams. Today we are more coy and use the Latin term, perhaps anglicising it to fellation or opting for ambiguous slang like 'blow job'. Prostitutes call it 'French'. Porn mags label it 'O' for oral sex. Personally, I prefer to call it cocksucking – I've always called a spade a spade.

Just how was it invented? If intercourse was learned from the birds and bees, then oral sex came surely from watching dogs and cats. Maybe Adam and Eve didn't latch on to it, but surely Mr and Mrs Noah did, with nowhere to go in the rain. Of course, it can even involve animals. We all know the tales about old ladies and Pekinese. The latest horror story concerns a horse. . . . A seaside photographer developed some holidaymaker's sunny snaps only to find a shot of a horse being given a blow job. Naturally, he blew it up large as a poster for the dark-room to inspire all his staff.

Is fellation *really* 'the most delicious meal', as a slightly androgynous male poet of my acquaintance describes it, or is it just a boring one-sided affair? That depends whether you're the sucker or on the receiving end. It also depends even more on whether you're a man or a woman. Fellation is frequently the subject of letters in girlie mags: 'I just love giving my boyfriend a blow job and feeling his warm sperm trickle down my throat. I can't get enough of his mammoth 12-inch cock.' Of course half these are written by the sort of blokes who have a kink about writing letters signed 'Mandy' or 'Samantha'.

Such magazines also advertise dolls with open mouths for lonely men. You used to see the disembodied heads of the cheap varieties, mouth a red O, lined up in sex shops before the barriers went up and the sign of adult toys became sheets of plywood rather than goodies in the windows. Of course, if you want the rest of the body you have to pay more. Now dolls are advertised in the *Sunday Sport* – 'BRIGITTE, life size de-luxe love doll, with 3 inviting entrances, open mouth, £70' or 'SUCKING LOVE DOLLS, inflatable, choice of 3, Chinese, black or blonde, £24.99.' If you're the James Bond type you might go for all three.

My first encounter with the concept of fellation in *real* life was at the age of ten. I used to go to a park in Acton to play and talk dirty with the other kids. There was a girl of about seven there who always dressed in pink. She used to disappear into the Gents with various older boys. 'She sucks their willies,' I was told. At the time I didn't even connect this with sex. Sex, I thought, was purely intercourse and happened between grown-ups who were married and wanted to have babies. I couldn't imagine why anyone would want to suck a willy. I found the concept rather disgusting – like eating worms. I went home and told my mother, who said, 'Ugh! That doesn't sound very nice, does it?' and assumed I'd made it all up. It's probably a mercy she didn't believe me, otherwise she'd have had to put the whole police and social services mechanism into motion. The girl would almost certainly have been institutionalised, which would probably have done her a lot more harm than sucking a few cocks. It's a shame I couldn't have interviewed the little cocksucker for this article. Did she do it for love of it? Or did she get a bag of sweeties? I'd hazard a guess it was the latter.

When I was fourteen I came on the subject again, labelled under the Latin word *fellatio* in a book I'd been lent. We used to swap smut to read under our desks in class. A lot of the girls in my school were doctors' daughters and could always provide good stuff. I can't remember which book it was in – it probably wasn't one of the usual medical textbooks because it went on to describe the taste of semen as 'a bit like weak milky coffee'. I've always remembered that. It also quoted an old wives' tale about swallowing semen to enlarge the size of the breasts. Of course there's a little protein in semen, but probably not as much as

there is in a Big Mac or a ploughman's lunch, and what adver-
tiser in their right mind would dare claim as much for these?

I was beginning to hear jokes on the subject too. At the time I
was going to a rather down-market Polish dentist who loved
my father's stories. Eventually the good relationship foundered
when my father told him the following one. A man went to a
dentist and said, 'Can you remove teeth from anywhere?' The
dentist said 'Yes', so the man pulled out his cock, showing a
double set of teeth embedded in it, and asked, 'Please remove
these.' The Polish dentist was furious and we all had to find
another dentist faster than a set of dentures can be extracted
from a cock, which was just as well for the future of our own
teeth.

It took a few years before I got on to the real thing. I was a late
starter with boys because of religious scruples. I don't think,
though, judging from friends' talk, that fellation would have
come into teenage sex – that is, unless the girls who did it
couldn't bear to talk about it. In some ways it's still a taboo
subject. When I published a poem in the *London Review of Books*
that mentioned 'the little cocksucker in pink' who haunted that
Acton park, a religious maniac wrote to the editor saying that if
he continued to publish my poems (a) he would cancel his sub
and (b) God would strike him dead. God, seemingly, had better
things to do. Karl Miller continued to publish and the man
continued to subscribe, presumably in case he missed any other
poems about cocksuckers.

I had my first taste of cocksucking with my first experience of
sex. About 50 per cent of men want it, I find. I was busy trying
to hide my inexperience so I went along with everything. I kept
that attitude for the first year or two of my sex life. For the next
few years I opted for pleasing only myself. In that period I came
across men who'd say, 'Just try it. I'm sure you'd like it. . . .' I'd
say I had and I didn't particularly, which surprised them a lot.
A good many men suffer from what I call the Phallic Worship
Syndrome. Those with PWS are convinced that women adore
big cocks in some almost religious sense and want to kneel
down before them, kiss and suck them. A cock only needs to be

serviceable. In my experience the hugely endowed make by far the worst lovers – they are so busy posing, waiting to have it admired, that they forget to do anything to please their partner. Looked at logically I can't see why men would think there is anything in fellation for the woman. Her mouth is better stimulated by the average kiss and unless the situation is turned into a 69 the rest of her body is left out in the cold. I have never read that semen is an aphrodisiac, whereas a woman's love juice, or whatever you call it, is supposed to be so. Perfume manufacturers spend a lot trying to synthesise it. Cunnilingus therefore is one up on a blow job. Even so, I wouldn't assume that every man wanted to perform it, in the way that men assume we're all panting to suck their cocks given half a chance.

So what *does* semen taste of? 'Weak milky coffee'? Possibly, if it's very weak – the coffee, I mean. Or perhaps puréed cucumber or white of egg? But I may be thinking more of the appearance. Perhaps it tastes of nothing at all, or little more than sweat or saliva.

In recent years I've come round to the view that you please yourself more if you spend part of the time trying to please others. Sucking's OK as an extension of kissing and mouthing other parts of the body – an animal kind of caress – but going on and on until somebody comes is another matter. When you're sucking away it can feel like eternity. I can't say I've used a stop-watch, but there's no doubt in my mind that fellation is the slowest way to make a partner come – considerably slower than intercourse. It's opposite to cunnilingus in this respect. Besides, too much sucking makes your face ache – like learning to play the recorder. If you're not the most patient of women you feel like saying, 'Come on, I haven't got all day!' I'm surprised prostitutes bother with it. They must lose a few tricks in the time.

I always thought it odd that fellation is called a 'blow job' not a 'suck job' until a male friend who's particularly into it explained that the best thrills were given by blowing and sucking alternately. (If you've got some ice-cream handy, so much the better.) It all helps the circulation at the sensitive end of the penis, apparently. Equivalent to our own slang 'blow job' is the Chinese phrase *p'in hsiao*, which means 'playing the flute'. German seems to have a similar expression. A poet friend of mine was taught rhymes in several languages as a child. He had to recite them to amuse his mother's friends at parties. The translation of the German one went, 'You can't have your sausage and play your flute at once.' Judging by the way the more cosmopolitan guests laughed he feels it must have meant something else.

It's amazing how little there is about cocksucking in Western literature. It doesn't seem to occur in old court cases either. Ordinary rape, yes; oral rape, no. Modern lawyers dealing with oral rape have to choose their words carefully. A barrister I once met brought the house down in Hastings County Court and got himself lampooned in *Punch* for saying that such a case 'left a nasty taste'. Until recently mention of oral sex made elderly judges' hair stand on end. Though it was never illegal, like anal sex between a man and a woman, it came under the heading of nasty practices that wives were made to submit to by husbands they later divorced for cruelty. When Ronald True was tried for strangling a prostitute, his argument that he acted in self-defence because he believed she was about to bite his cock off in the bath damned him immediately in the eyes of the judge and jury.

Fellation is beginning to make an appearance in popular culture now the taboos are fading. Lou Reed's song 'Sister Ray' has the refrain 'Too busy sucking on my ding dong'. There is also the Andy Warhol short *Blow Job*, which shows 'a young man's face as he experiences fellatio'. Nonetheless, the major source of references to fellation is still Latin poetry. The Romans thoroughly despised those who practised it. *Fellat* (he/she sucks cocks) was the worst possible thing you could say about anyone. It occurs in many epigrams. (Translators of several decades ago preferred to render it by the less comprehensible 'he sucks'.) Since my mother and I translated some Martial epigrams *fellat* has become a family joke. We shout it at our old tom cat. He has come to recognise the word too, and stops mid-suck whenever he hears it. To suck yourself must be the ultimate narcissistic thrill. I once met a theatre usher who claimed, 'I could do it if I wanted to.' He had a very flexible back.

After Roman times, European literature seems to have steered clear of the subject until the present century. Oriental literature, on the other hand, is a lot more frank. *The Arabian Nights*, I'm told, had its moments in the original Sir Richard Burton translation. Unfortunately, Lady Burton had got to work on the family edition I own, so I can't verify this. The classic early seventeenth-century Chinese novel *Chin P'ing Mei* certainly contains a lot of cocksucking. Golden Lotus, the heroine, even goes into the realm of 'watersports' and swallows a whole bladderful of pee to save her swain the effort of getting out of bed during an all-night session of fellation. With typical male idiocy, Hsi-men, the hero, asks if it tastes good. 'It tastes a little alkaline. I would like to have fragrant tea leaves to take the taste away,' she replies. Instead of being the perfect gent and making her a cuppa, Hsi-men tells her to help herself to a few leaves from the pocket of his white silk jacket, which is hanging on the bedpost.

Talking to friends, male and female, while trying to write this article has proved a revelation. One of them bravely increased the numbers in my mini-survey by asking questions all round her office. It proved to be a great conversation-stopper, she complained. Those normally garrulous became silent for the first time in years. I got a similar silence from a visitor last week. He asked what I was writing about and I told him. Being a shy bachelor of sheltered upbringing he had to have the word 'fellation' explained. I did this rather cleanly, I thought, by saying, 'Sucking men off.' I couldn't have said 'blow job' to this old-fashioned character; he'd have thought it was something to do with a hairdresser's or a vacuum cleaner. My poor embarrassed visitor turned a nasty shade of beetroot, crossed his legs tightly to stop me committing oral rape and sat silent for a while.

At the end of my research amongst friends and acquaintances, I have to say that I simply cannot find a woman like the heroines of porn novels – one who actually enjoys, rather than just puts up with, sucking cocks. Sixty-nines are fine, but not blow jobs in isolation. When it comes down to it it's men who really enjoy fellation – sucking as well as being sucked. It's a part of homosexual culture. Come to think of it, the bulk of the Roman epigrams referred to homosexual episodes. The Romans had no taboo about homosexuality *per se*, only with regard to the part-ner providing the orifice. Orton shows a similar contemptuous attitude when he refers to 'queens' as 'she'. There's plenty about cocksucking in his highly enjoyable Diary. Ironically, for a master of black comedy, the last sexual experience he re-corded before his murder was fellation by an unknown dwarf while another man watched in a Brighton lavatory: 'He made a motion to the dwarfish creature, rather as someone would call a taxi. The dwarf sucked me off while the other man smiled benevolently.'

Men who are homosexual or who have had some homosexual experiences are probably most open about oral sex. A great many will talk with enthusiasm about it and say they prefer it to anal sex. In these days of AIDS I expect this will increasingly become the case. A bisexual friend of mine told me the tale of 'Toothless George', who was in great demand on Jersey. Having it done by someone toothless is supposed to be quite desirable, because there's no need to fear being bitten. 'Toothless George' from Blackpool used to spend three months a year holidaying on Jersey. Every day he'd go out on to the rocks and suck off anyone who wanted it – not for money, just for the love of it. It's nice to know that the old and toothless have some use. Psychologists like to talk about men's fear of the 'vagina dentata' but it's remarkable how few men in practice fear women's mouths. I once met a tooth-fetishist Italian who actually wanted his cock bitten. Toothless George (or Georgina) would have been a grave disappointment to him.

Men are attracted by images of fellation. Many prostitutes advertise with phrases like 'Sexy Lips' or 'Pouting Lips'. There is now a poster showing a woman sucking a banana. I have a feeling I may be indirectly responsible for the latter. About fifteen years ago, while commuting on the London tube, I got so bored that I started to put on little acts. Sucking a banana proved the most popular and was generally irresistible to the man opposite, especially if I wore bright red lipstick and stared into his eyes while doing so. One night I tried a carrot instead; the sharp crunch of teeth through vegetable only made men nervous, so there must be something to the old 'vagina dentata' theory, after all.

No article on blow jobs would be complete without a mention of Linda Lovelace, star of *Deep Throat*. In pornospiel, the name Linda has become almost synonymous with a woman who sucks cocks. Chat lines on fellation have titles like 'LIQUID LIPS supplied by Linda' or 'LINDA'S GOT HER MOUTHFUL, find out why'. I read what's supposed to be Linda Lovelace's auto-biography years ago. I say *supposed* because I have serious doubts about whether this book can have been written by a woman. In fact, Linda Lovelace, when on a chat show, talked of being exploited and having words put into her mouth. While I can buy insatiability in a woman's autobiography, I can't seriously believe that anyone goes down the supermarket with a vibrator or two thrumming away inside her. The book elaborated on the technique of 'deep throat', swallowing the whole of a man's cock rather than just sucking the end. It was compared to sword-swallowing, something that had to be learned. The body has to be positioned with the head tipped back so that the throat is aligned and at its most open. What the book didn't point out, of course, is that it's diabolically dangerous, even more so than sword-swallowing. OK, cocks don't have a cutting edge, but then they *are* thicker than the average sword. Even if you can manage to get them past your tonsils without gagging, they could block the airway. Is the excited bloke who's thrusting away going to notice if the woman concerned turns blue because she can no longer breathe? I doubt it. Deep throat is only for psychopaths, in my opinion, and should not be put up with by any woman either for love or for money. I can see a good case for fellation as a preliminary turn-on, especially to encourage those who have a tendency towards impotence to take a firm stand, but if a man's up and thrusting what's wrong with a woman's cunt – a part that's decidedly more elastic?

I draw the line at deep throat. I also draw it at sucking a condom. Years ago, I jokingly compared eating whelks – the only form of seafood I don't like – to trying to chew through a pint of condomed cocks, never dreaming then that anyone would use condoms for oral sex. Yet since the AIDS scare manufacturers have cashed in by producing flavoured ones, strawberry, orange, etc. *Chacun à son gout.* I can't think of anything less erotic. I doubt if the man gets anything out of it either. Someone I once met – a voluntary helper at an AIDS advisory service – told me that there were no known cases of the virus being passed on by fellation, anyway. It seems to me that such condoms will be used only by prostitutes who don't fancy (in the sense of being squeamish about as well as being unattracted by) the bloke they're sucking and are twice as bored by the operation as other women.

Why do ordinary women suck cocks when they do not really enjoy it? Like the prostitute we're doing it for something in return. In her case it's money, in ours it's some reciprocal demonstration of affection: cunnilingus, perhaps, or a bout of good sex, after or before – a quid pro quo. These are the real reasons. The reasons given in pornography are different. One of the lovers of the man of letters and fuck-and-tell boaster Frank Harris (the author of *My Life and Loves*) gives him his first blow job: 'Your seed, darling, is dear to me. I don't want it in my sex; I want to feel you thrill and so I want your sex in my mouth, I want to drink your essence and I will. . . .' (Do women ever talk like that?) Afterwards she says, 'Wait till some girl does that to you and you'll know she loves you to distraction or better still to self-destruction.' *Chin P'ing Mei* theorises similarly that it's something courtesans do to bind men to them more than to their wives. Love doesn't necessarily go with fellation any more than it does with sex. It might, but it also might not. All I've ever felt during both straight and oral sex was some temporary affection and lust. Those are good enough reasons. I don't believe, either, that being sucked produces any kind of enslavement in the man. The chapters that follow Frank Harris's blow job show just how little enslavement or love entered into that situation. By the next fuck with his cocksucker he was thinking of another woman and comparing her unfavourably. Her affection lasted a bit longer, but not a lot. When he didn't pay her enough attention she got herself another toy-boy.

To men everywhere I'd say that if you're lucky enough to get a woman instead of a vibrating sex doll to suck you off, don't kid yourself she's loving every minute, or that she loves you *necessarily*. Look at the situation realistically and tell yourself, 'This nice woman's putting up with a lot of boredom for my sake. The least I can do is show my gratitude in one way or another.'

Advice to Young Poets

'Don't put your daughter on the stage', the song runs. Mrs Worthington would probably be given the same advice about poetry. Yet, properly handled, it can be a good career, even a lucrative one. Poetry should be thought of as a profession comparable to the law or medicine. Doctors and barristers need a long training during which they earn little if anything, but afterwards there are substantial rewards. To be successful both in terms of fame and wealth, poets have to run their careers as a business. Put in forty hours a week, and remember, deadlines are important. If poets play on their unworldliness, like women admitting to PMT, they define themselves as inferior. Have visions by all means, but have them in your own time and deliver the goods at the end of the day.

So what should Mrs Worthington's daughter expect if she goes in for poetry? The literary world's a game of snakes and ladders with the emphasis on the snakes. On the way up you'll be treated with contempt. Once you're known it's jealousy-time, and there's a Freemason-like process of initiation on the way to success. First comes ordeal by small mags that don't pay. When you start submitting work, be prepared for the rough treatment to begin. Those who edit poetry magazines and run specialist publishing houses are not always the kindest people. Some enjoy stealing the obligatory stamped addressed envelopes. Others take a year before deigning to send you a note of unparalleled nastiness. I once even received the contents of a waste-paper basket in return for my poems. I spent a year and a half sending work out and clocked up eighty-six rejections before one poem was taken in a non-paying magazine. Some editors more or less demand subscriptions before they'll consider your work.

The good thing about this tough apprenticeship is that it thickens the skin so much that bad reviews will not hurt, when you get to that stage. The problem is, though, that the poet has to survive in the meantime. Part-time or casual jobs are best. In my case I chose odd days of teaching or film-extra work, or the dole when even those failed. A full-time job kills a poet's talent – eventually. You can't treat the muse as a bit on the side with impugnity. Jeremy Reed puts the dilemma succinctly in his fine critical work *Madness – The Price of Poetry*: 'If one were to ask an accountant to work as a ticket-collector in the afternoons, he would protest that it was a violation of his profession. A poet, however, is expected to be everything but a poet.'

From small magazines the poet graduates to small presses. At last there is something that looks like a book – or more or less like one, in some cases. It took me six years to reach this stage. I was also contributing to the odd anthology and had started to win light-verse competitions in the *New Statesman* and *The Spectator*. You can also try major poetry competitions too. The odds are several thousand to one against winning, though, and could in fact be more stacked than you think. One judge told me he always looks for the work of his friends. Unfortunately I had quarrelled with him at the time. Judges do, of course, recognise the style of a known poet in anonymous submissions. This year's Arvon prize (£5,000) is to be judged by publishers. In my view the practice of employing publishers as judges is a questionable one. However fair they try to be, they have a financial interest in seeing that writers on their lists win. There is also the possibility that they may have seen the work submitted before. A competition usually requires unpublished submissions, but publishers have a poet's work in hand a year before publication.

From light-verse competitions, I began to see the possibilities for a more serious kind of satire. My new poems often criticised men, but the masochists took to them. I began to get work into magazines my friends had heard of – the *New Statesman* and the *London Review of Books*. Both paid reasonably and I didn't get threatening letters from their editors demanding subscriptions. Once you are publishing in nationally distributed magazines you stand a chance of having a book taken by a mainstream publisher.

Editors are cautious beasts. By the middle of 1985, after seven years in the business, I had completed enough work in the new style for a collection, the *Sky Ray Lolly* poems, which I sent to Chatto and Windus. Andrew Motion, the Poetry Editor, rejected it but suggested a meeting. Over lunch he worked his courage up to asking if the poems were true. Of course they are. I thought at the time that Andrew just wanted a look at the monster who'd dared to describe male organs disparagingly. But no, it was only partly that. He wanted a second read of the collection. Publishers have a strange attitude towards poetry. They like to publish a little for prestige, but will not pay a decent rate for it. It is still thought all right for them to offer advances of less than a thousand pounds to quite successful poets. They would never dream of offering as little for a first novel. This is unreasonable, because poetry does not sell any worse than first novels, and top-selling poets like Seamus Heaney can shift 30,000 copies.

The sad truth is that most publishers are simply taking advantage of poets. Chatto and Windus paid me only a stingy 5 per cent royalty on the two poetry books they published. My advances for *Sky Ray Lolly* and *Private Parts* were £200 and £400. Of course writers are not expected to derive all their income from sales alone. Once your book is out and reviewed, readings become an option. A writer is a fool to do these for free, since the amount of travelling involved often takes you away for two days at a time. A hundred pounds is a sensible fee, and anything less than £50 is inadequate. If at all possible a writer should insist on hotel accommodation. Family hospitality can be like a one-night stand without the sex.

Apart from publishers there are the organisations that are *meant* to be of use to poets. In my years of greatest financial need, I tried in turn the Poetry Society, the British Council, the Society of Authors and the Arts Council. The first two wouldn't give me a single reading. The others weren't interested in help-ing me with any kind of award. The Society of Authors is responsible for the Gregory Awards, which are specifically for poets under thirty. The first vetting was done by Howard

Sergeant in the days when I was young enough to try; he was a
judge on a great many literary competitions in his lifetime. The
awards have had a stinkingly poor record on equality. I have
complained about the Gregory Trust to the Charity Commission, but they tell me that it's up to the trustees. The
trustees are the judges – so who keeps the keepers? The statis-
tics relating to past competition winners are telling. It would
seem that black writers stand almost no chance of winning. The
situation for women is little better. Only twenty-two out of 153
awards have gone to women. Most of the reasonably well-
known women poets around today – Carol Rumens, Wendy
Cope, myself, to name but a few – have not had them. In my
own case, it was certainly not for lack of trying; I was turned
down six times. Interestingly the one reasonably known
woman poet who's received a Gregory award previously published a booklet with Howard Sergeant's vanity-press periodical
Outposts. Howard Sergeant's approach to poetry was not one I
could admire.

The other main awards are given by the Arts Council. I fear I
will never be able to try for one of these again while Dr Alastair
Niven is a judge. When I recently sued the Arts Council for
discrimination, he told the court, 'She'll have a fair chance of an
award, *until* her work is read.' The *Sunday Times* had previously
reported an 'arts councillor' as saying that the only prizes I'd
win were 'of the cattle-market variety'. Maybe I should put a
bell round my neck and low through Niven's letter-box.

In the absence of awards, it was financially essential that I
find a publisher prepared to pay me a decent price for my
poetry. A lot of people have asked me why I was so stupid as to
accept Chatto's 5 per cent contracts. The answer is that I did not
know any better. Writers don't talk much about their fees. A
little asking around showed me that most of Chatto's poets
were getting the same, even more experienced writers. It was
finding out that 5 per cent was not a proper rate that made me
change publisher. My aggressive and unusual way of doing so
was one of the things that helped my career most.

Before the new collection was finished and before I had a new publisher, I burned my boats by breaking with the old one publicly. I wrote a poem called 'Prostitution' in which all the facts about my income and what Chatto had paid me were declared. I compared their role to that of an oppressive pimp. Worse still, I recited the poem on Channel Four's *Comment*. The producer rang my publishers to make sure they had a nice surprise on telly that evening.

I believe it's the duty of a poet of integrity to improve the literary world for all. That is why I make trouble when I find injustices. It's a great pity that there's not more solidarity amongst poets. Even a little openness would do. Last year I met a German photographer who told me a significant story. Photographers, he said, were badly paid in Germany, *until* they got together and told each other what they earned. After that they were able to get good fixed rates for their work. Writers are in the position of those German photographers several years ago. Most of us are not very well off, so we don't like to declare our incomes. On the other hand, it is against our own interests to hide facts such as what advances and what royalties we get. If we could be good friends to each other and exchange these snippets of information, we could all obtain better deals. That is the reason that I am choosing to quote facts and figures about who pays what. It is worth putting on record both successes and failures.

Not surprisingly, after the 'Prostitution' poem, it took me several months to find a new publisher. Both OUP and Secker refused to look at the new collection. I tried my work on Craig Raine for Faber, but he advised me to go back to Chatto. Poetic friends made the same suggestion, and humble pie was mentioned. But I was finished with 5 per cent contracts. About the same time I advertised in the *London Review of Books* for an agent and wrote a letter to their pages stating my needs as a writer. Like my piece on television it quoted facts and figures. All I wanted was to be allowed to make a living.

I got an agent via my advert. Agents are a must for a writer. Publishers take you more seriously and the price you get for a book is better; but, like publishers, they are choosy. Four had turned me down previously. When Giles Gordon answered my advertisement and took me on, he suggested the unprecedented step of auctioning my new collection at the Frankfurt Book Fair. Top bidder for *The Perfect Man* was Julian Evans of Abacus with £10,500. I nearly fainted when I heard the good news over the phone, and went round with an unholy grin on my face for weeks. It proved to me that some publishers at any rate are prepared to pay a proper sum for a poetry book. I have tried to confirm my £10,500 advance as an all-time record for poetry, but Norris McWhirter hasn't answered my letter.

Macho Feminists

Society has suffered much at the hands of macho men. Now there is a new breed – macho women. One feminist decrees we are not to like sex, then expects her sisters to follow. If another says that women who show their tits for a living should be written off, then again we must follow. Male preachers have been damning sex and nudity for centuries. How familiar it all sounds.

I believe passionately in freedom. I must therefore recognise the right of any individual of either sex to wear (or not wear) make-up, tights, stockings, bras, corsets, high or low heels, long hair, short hair, minis, maxis, saucy underwear and the rest.

I am also a feminist. I want to see women having equal pay, equal job opportunities and equal rights of all kinds. I want to see women priests and an end to Salic law. A discussion with some like-minded women in my local sauna came up with a unanimous verdict that Anne should be next in line to the throne after Charles. She would certainly handle it better than little Prince Willy. I want to see rape victims treated as fairly as the victims of burglary. How often do the police ask the latter if they wanted to have their goods stolen or if they've ever given any away in the past? I want to see better child-care facilities and allowances. Alternatively, if the Government finds this too costly, I would like to see the having of children held against men as much as women in employment. 'Oh no, we can't make him bank manager. He'll only go and have a baby in a year or two. . . .'

Equal rights are important. The exposure of flesh, on the other hand, is not. I trained as a painter before taking up writing. I drew nudes, male and female, over a period of seven years. Perhaps that's why I can't evince any shock at them. The artists' models I talked to then mostly felt exploited. Both men and women were paid about 50p an hour in the early seventies.

I knew girls at art school, on the other hand, who posed once or twice for nude photos at a much higher rate. They didn't feel exploited as they had been paid an adequate amount of money for the job.

I don't love Page 3, but for reasons of freedom I don't want to ban it. Censorship of any kind is a dubious weapon. If we get rid of Page 3 and Miss World, where do we draw the next line? I have taken up weight-training as a hobby. Some of the other women who work out at the local sports centre enjoy going in for bodybuilding competitions. These are officially designated a sport and yet the format and the titles make them very much like standard beauty contests. Is a woman who flexes her muscles in a bikini in front of a large audience also setting back the cause of women a million years? I have never come across any feminist dicta on this subject.

As an ex-artist who's profoundly interested in the human form in all its permutations, I would like to see such competitions continue. I would prefer it, though, if the prurient elements were removed. Competitions should be held completely naked and be for both sexes. I would like beauty or physique to be the scoring factors. The element I find sickening in pageants is when beauty queens have to come out with a contrived spiel about how they are going to help the handicapped or work with children. That kind of stereotyping could well be harmful to women. Having to be nice, right-minded and caring has kept us under-paid for years.

How far should papers go in banning Page 3-type photos to appease those who are offended by them? Would it be OK if the tits were partially covered? I'd hazard a guess that any ban would breed a host of new prurient pictures delighting in almost breaking the rules. A hundred years or more ago men got their kicks in public from seeing a flash of ankle or a touch of knicker leg. Nude photographs were to be passed round among gentlemen, not to be seen by their wives in daily newspapers. Yet Queen Victoria's reign, with its veneer of moral values, was a time of massive child prostitution.

Nudity does not amount to a nuclear war. To use the force of feminism against it is to sidestep more important issues. Censorship could well be a better target. Some lesbians made a memorable protest against the infamous Clause 28 in the House of Lords. Protest or no, the bill went through. It was passed, Baroness Turner, the Employment Spokeswoman, told me, because the Government brought in all the old peers who usually never vote. Now, if feminists want a real cause to fight for – how about some changes in the House? If a few of the old codgers who can't be bothered to turn up were given the sack and a few sensible women brought in, who knows what difference it might make to us all next time an important issue like child benefit is debated? Feminism should be concerned with equal pay and equal rights, not reinforcing old limitations.

Platonic Friendship

A man or woman can do many things alone. I prefer to travel and go to the theatre, opera and exhibitions this way. I choose to do so because I like to take things at my own speed and form my own opinions uninfluenced by anyone else. It's a saddening experience to come out of an opera bursting with enthusiasm, only to find your friend can do nothing but laugh at the fat prima donna. But I still like to meet friends from time to time for a chat over a meal or drinks. My oldest friends I've known since primary school. News of more recent events can be exchanged knowing we have a long bank of past shared experience to draw on.

These friends are women, as I went to a single-sex school. I sometimes regret having had that sort of education. As girls we all sniggered at boys and thought of them as sex objects in the way men are supposed to think of women. Sharing our classes with the other sex would have given us a better idea of the world outside. I had no inkling of the prejudice I would be subjected to until I started trying for work and submitting articles to magazines.

Some of my more recent friends have been men. I am cautious about taking on new friends, though. I am anxious not to fritter away my time. I have had many affairs without any friendship element simply because I feel I would have been bored to death if I'd had to listen to the men concerned for any length of time. I am more careful about acquiring friends than lovers. The phrase 'platonic friendship' is most often used to mean one between the sexes that does not include sex, although the word derives from the name of Plato, the homosexual, adoring friend and biographer of Socrates. Victorians who admired his writing liked to believe he sublimated any feelings he had for Socrates and the handsome younger philosophers who swarmed around him.

I am inclined to agree with the French, who have a proverb

about friendship between men and women being only for the old and the sick. When I'm old, maybe I'll find such friendships more possible than I do now. Socialising with a group of men at work is all right. You can all have a drink afterwards, then go your separate ways. I like drinking with a bunch of men. I am the centre of attention and can come out with a good line in Mae West-type jokes. It brings out the best in me. It's pleasant also to know a few people to chat to at a party. A more serious friendship – the sort where you go out to meet someone or have them back to your home – rarely works on a long-term basis. I've had a few platonic relationships with men, but these have never lasted as long as my friendships with women. Where I entered such situations hoping for an affair, the friendships ended in bitterness. I feel young and attractive and I resent it if a man who takes me out doesn't want to make love to me. I start to dislike him thoroughly, telling myself he must be impotent or a homosexual without the guts to own up to what he is. There seem to be quite a few of these time-wasting flirts around in England. I haven't worked out whether it's the climate or heredity. It's certainly a condition that foreign men seem less prone to. It's very comforting when you're with a man who only wants one thing. You know exactly where you are.

Platonic friendships function well enough, I find, when the man is either exclusively homosexual or a great deal older than myself. In these situations I am able to rule out the question of sex completely. We are no more to each other than a couple of heterosexual women going for a drink and sharing confidences – perhaps discussing our affairs or what shampoo to use. In fact the friendships with homosexuals work best of all because homosexuals are never moralistic. Older men can be.

If a male friend marries or lives with someone, this can put another kind of strain on the situation. You have two options – either to walk away or be friends with both. In the case of an artist friend of mine, this wasn't difficult. I like his new live-in girlfriend, who's a singer. Because I've studied singing a little we can talk about that. Her singing and performing side is the part she can't really share with him.

Friendships with other women can also become difficult once a partner's involved. Couples and singles are not an easy mix. I feel particularly *de trop* staying with a couple. Families always have their own special jokes, and a guest is an intruder. It's better to meet your coupled friends on neutral ground like a pub or restaurant. Also, a single woman is often seen as a possible marauder. Your friend's lover may be about as fanciable as Frankenstein, but because she picked him up she'll assume you're just as undiscriminating.

The rule in keeping friends of any kind seems to be tolerance. I don't criticise my long-term friends' habits or partners. I hope they won't criticise mine. When we get together we usually have a good bitch about others. That can be very rewarding as long as you're sure none of it will be repeated afterwards. It's important too to admire other people's triumphs. You may not understand what her promotion means, but admire it; boring holiday snaps likewise.

Women friends are a necessity because there are times when it is hard to confide completely in someone of another sex. I'm not a modest shrinking violet so I'm prepared to share rude jokes and intimate facts with a man quite readily. On the other hand the basic biological differences between the sexes mean that it is often not possible for men and women to empathise with one another. I once said to a man friend that I preferred having an internal examination with a female doctor because a woman understood the angle of the vagina better and didn't attempt a macho thrust. A woman would have known exactly what I meant. I was probably similarly lacking in understanding when he told me a little about some trouble with his prostate gland. If you don't have a certain part you can't understand the psychological and physiological problems attached. Conversations about cystitis and thrush are for women to share with women. Prostate and erectile problems are a case for male sympathies only.

There's another side to these medical talks too. You can't help wondering whether the person concerned is talking intimately about themselves to turn you on. I was very much attracted to an older man who used to take me out – not for sex, but to talk.

I heard all about his urinary and potency problems. At least half of any conversation was taken up with discussing his penis. When it wasn't that it was his unhappy marriage or other affairs. I would have been quite happy to talk about his penis or what a bitch his wife was for hours if only I'd had some tangible benefit out of the situation. That platonic friendship proved to be a deeply frustrating and extremely annoying one, and I ended up feeling thoroughly used. If I'd been his psychologist instead of his friend I'd certainly have made several thousand out of him in fees.

Traditionally men are supposed to keep a stiff upper lip at all times. Yet women are often disarmed by those who can cry and express human insecurities. Such men can make good friends. A sense of humour about these insecurities is very attractive. I once heard an illuminating tale of how a man couldn't stand using the Gents. He couldn't face peeing in front of other men, and was afraid he wouldn't be able to manage it while standing next to 'some great oaf in full flood'. Instead he used to retire into a cubicle, kick the seat up and avoid touching anything in case he found traces of 'slime'. (Women, of course, don't go as far as that – they just cover everything in toilet paper because their mums told them they might catch VD from the seat.) My friend's story was interesting because it emphasised the basic oneness of men and women. Women aren't expected to urinate in front of each other – why should men be?

Apart from certain bodily parts men have a lot in common with women. I feel that the differences are often too much exaggerated. The traditional views of male and female roles are crude generalisations at best. There's a large area of common ground to be discussed, and it is useful to an understanding of human nature to search out the points where male and female sensibilities overlap. Perhaps the only way to fight the prejudice of sexism is by gaining a deeper understanding of the other sex's similarities and differences. Some degree of friendship is necessary for that.

Le Weekend

Contrary to popular belief, I have never been on a dirty weekend with anyone. Perhaps it's because my relationships usually don't last that long. Have I missed out? It's an experience that seems to be getting rarer and rarer for every body these days. In fact, I've only met a few people who'll admit to having had one.

However much they are planned and looked forward to, dirty weekends rarely go smoothly. When I was a student, a pair of friends who were living with their parents booked into a country hotel. For days before, the bloke kept saying, 'It's costing me, but oh, it'll be worth it.' He said it so often that some of us started using it as a catchphrase. When they reached their destination, his girlfriend suffered a severe bout of asthma and had to be kept by the fire, cradling her inhaler. More recently a poet friend of mine was giving a reading in Norfolk. He brought someone along on the basis that most of the expenses – except her rail fare – could be pushed on to the Arts Festival organisers while the two of them had a quiet dirty weekend in Cromer. But the Arts Centre went bust and he was left without even a fee for his reading – a piece of poetic justice, in my opinion. Men often prefer toying with the idea of a weekend rather than the expensive actuality. The same poet went to a literary lunch where I was giving a speech and enjoyed standing at the hotel desk, with me by his side, asking about the price of rooms. Nothing came of it, of course.

I live in Hastings. Some would say it's the poor relative of Brighton, the traditional home of the dirty weekend. In theory the IRA bombing should have shifted the trade to other seaside towns, but it hasn't. Perhaps the local hotels aren't up to it. Only one of them goes in heavily for romance. Adverts boast of the four-poster and Nottingham lace in the honeymoon suite. Outside, in the garden, there are ornamental hens for 'the kiddies' to play with. Hastings is not big on water-beds and tiger-skins, but things may change – it is rumoured that Cynthia Payne is moving down.

Now that sex is no longer labelled 'dirty', some whizz-kid should think of a new name for the dirty weekend to get the tourist trade rolling again – perhaps 'Le Weekend'. Proprietors of hotels would need to develop a more sophisticated approach than at present. A literary friend of mine went to a small place in Rye with the woman he's since married. All weekend long, he swears, staff came to have a nudge-nudge, wink-wink, sniggering look at them – and they hadn't even registered as Mr and Mrs Smith.

Even if hotels can't get it right, there's the private version of the dirty weekend. Doing it in your own home avoids the thorny equality question of who pays. As a workaholic I can see a lot of point to seeing a lover at weekends only. The anticipation and planning could be fun. Five working days might also be useful to get yourself looking your best. You could both spend the week saunaing, exercising, dieting, dyeing your grey hairs, whatever it takes, then meet up none the wiser about all the effort that's gone into the other person's appearance.

Hastings has a lot to offer holidaymakers who are romantically inclined: aphrodisiac seafood of every kind, and quaint Elizabethan houses that would blow American minds. For the more down-to-earth, there's the inspirational sight of seagulls doing it everywhere. For the older generation there are local productions of such musical gems as *The King and I*. The more cynical might enjoy the parade of loonies along the prom; on a good day you can see anything from the Duke of Wellington on a bike to a blue nylon-fur shark who's advertising something (presumably). Mean couples can drive out to all the pick-your-own farms and come back laden with raspberries. Fit couples can make it to the nudist beach – a three-mile hike up hill and down dale across the Country Park.

Now I've moved out from Mum, dirty weekends at home seem a distinct possibility. After all, I'm offering the ultimate status symbol: a mistress with a cottage by the sea, complete with a French antique bed. Unfortunately, most of the men I meet socially are either gay or married. Married men can manage a dirty day-trip to Hastings without their wives being any the wiser, I find, but never a whole weekend.

Some Like It Hot

In the spring a young man's fancy lightly turns to thoughts of. . . . The sap is rising and the birds are nesting. All nature's at it. But then humans don't have a proper mating season. It's sometimes summer before Man can get his act together.

We all know that the British, bonking their way round Benidorm, are a friskier lot abroad than back home. A few gallons of cheap vino and plenty of Mediterranean sunshine and they're anybody's. (That is, if they can still manage it.) But is the sunshine alone enough to make us shed clothes and inhibitions together? Probably. Traditionally, heat has been associated with sex for so long that it's even passed into the language: hot stuff, hot pants, bitch in heat, people having the hots for each other. You can get your warmth from a large coal fire, central heating, a well-sealed igloo (Eskimos are supposed to be quite romantic), a few stiff whiskies or, more cheaply, from the sun when it deigns to shine on our cold shores.

One of the great things about summer is that it broadens your choice. You can find yourself a tourist toy-boy, here to learn the language; you're not stuck with the local talent. There are less clothes in summer to tear off in a fit of passion. And it's not only 'Your place or mine?' – couples can opt for the great outdoors if they can find a suitable spot. The fantasy of outdoor sex goes back to our first ancestors: Adam and Eve in the Garden of Eden, one with the animals and nature; couples rolling ecstatically in the waves in old movies without getting drowned or pebble-dashed. But the reality is often very different. A roll in the waves or the hay can cost you dear. For us paleskins there's the problem of sunburn if we frolic alfresco. We can always get our lovers to stroke on the calamine afterwards, but it's a bit of a masochist's massage, where every new position is sheer agony. Then there are the mosquitoes. . . .

After a few chilly years, Britain seems all set for a long hot summer. As the temperatures soar the clothes come off. We even have nudist beaches now. I live in the town that had the first – Hastings. The only problem is that to get to this beach you have to do an assault course across fields of mud. A friend of mine who visits there regularly – he's an artist, that's his excuse – tells me that it is singularly unerotic. All the couples on the beach are committed naturists and some are OAPs. He speaks distastefully of the sagged breasts, rolls of flab and skin like old handbags – alligator ones. Still, there must be something to the place. He keeps on going back.

I prefer a daily swim on the ordinary beach. Most of the people who sit there are very discreet. You don't get stared at. In fact, it's almost too discreet to be flattering. I've stripped off seductively in front of the open-air gospel meeting without a blind bit of notice being taken. You don't see much fooling around, either. But then, maybe only the exceptionally kinky would opt for love on a bed of British pebbles, not to mention what the local Rottweilers have added to it. A friend of mine once had a Cretan lorry driver on pebbles, but she said it wasn't to be recommended. Nor do I think much of sand – it gets in everything.

I have always felt randier in the summer. The sun gives a feeling of well-being. Thinner clothes sort out the attractive from the unattractive, so you can see exactly what you're getting. A paunch is a paunch in a T-shirt, but winter woolies are comparatively discreet. People are more sensible about the effects of the sun, too, than they used to be. A few years ago Brits didn't feel they'd had value from their holiday unless they came back red and blistered. Now, with the threat of skin cancer, things are changing. We're all slapping on the Factor 10 before we go sun-worshipping. Pale and interesting equals pale and healthy. Only the lightest of golden tans is fashionable.

In the last century, with all those stuffy clothes and layers of underwear, summer was probably hell. Their spotted muslins could have been cool, but not with ankle-length knickers, petticoats and corsets beneath. The Victorians were less in tune with the earth than any other century, and randiness was the thing

furthest from their minds. Their forefathers were very different.
Earlier clothing often involved an elaborate bodice for women,
but no knickers under the skirt. Men had breeches with laces
that could be undone quickly. Sex could be indulged in easily,
'any time, any place, anywhere', as the Martini ad goes. Pre-
nineteenth-century writers are much more explicit. It's interesting that a good deal of the sex that turns up in medieval poetry,
Elizabethan plays and novels of the eighteenth century is located out of doors and is of the rural romp or roll-in-the-hay
variety. It is therefore likely to have taken place in the warmer
part of the year. Real-life court cases of the past convey the
same impression. *Wanton Wenches and Wayward Wives* by
G.R. Quaife details peasant life using legal records from
seventeenth-century Somerset: 'A Taunton man thoroughly enjoyed himself at Broomfield Fair. As evening settled he discovered a very willing wench and began to have his way with
her against what must have appeared a reasonably firm tree. It
was in fact the ceremonial pole erected for the festival, and their
unrestrained sexual movements were such that they "made a
bell hanging on top of the pole to ring out, whereby he was . . .
discovered".' I can't see that happening on a British winter
night.

Standard Diary

One of my neighbours has been complaining because the large Victorian house on the corner will soon be filled with the mentally handicapped. Personally, I don't think you can better the mentally handicapped as neighbours. They don't have wild parties in the small hours, rev up bikes or own Porsches for the rest of us to envy.

I am also the sort of neighbour people don't like to have. I don't put on wild parties or the rest, but our house is the only one in the road with flaking paint, and a window-cleaner hasn't been near it for ten years. Worse still, I own a tom cat.

I was brought up properly, of course. All but one of the cats I had as a child were spayed or neutered. The one who escaped was a Siamese queen. We had hoped to make money out of her, but she had her own ideas about mates and preferred a surly black and white Manx cat with one and a half ears. Tess presented us with a total of sixty-six kittens, none of them pedigree ones. The expensive vet we used thought he saw traces of Siamese ancestry in the pads under one kitten's feet, but that was as close as we came. My father adored and trusted the vet, both for that piece of discernment and also for saying, of another of our cats, 'Little Binky shall not die!' Binky, the sole survivor of a runty litter, lived to the ripe old age of seventeen, her health sustained by surreptitious draughts from visitors' sherry glasses. But my father's faith in this vet was demolished when he heard that he was wintering in Florida. It was not that he begrudged him a holiday, but he was disillusioned by the Ansafone message: 'Dr Benjamin is on his rounds attending the sick and suffering. . . .'

My current cat, Peregrine Pickle, has no Siamese ancestry. I took him in when the people opposite did a moonlight flit owing six months' rent and leaving him to fend for himself. The old villain came, wet and crying, to my window in the midst of a Boris Karloff movie. His owners had told their poor deceived landlady that he had 'been done'. They always called him Whisky, and he will answer to that still, as well as to various swear words, or to his nickname, Grinner. I call him the Grinner because he has a white one-sided smile marked on his black face. The rest of his pot-bellied body has a sort of tuxedo effect like a waiter on the skids. Over the last few years I have seen a number of kittens with white smiles appearing in the district. They are all very good-natured, just like their old dad. Peregrine also has his own personal cat-door. I 'glazed' the basement lavatory window with an unwanted canvas of a male nude, leaving the corner unstapled so that he could force his way in or out. In fine weather he does his courting in the rockery at the end of the garden. He's a perfect gent – he always goes in for lots of foreplay. He also has Platonic friends, a couple of tortoiseshells, and just gives them a few whiskery kisses in the bushes. In the winter he brings other cats in for the night. The basement is turning into a kind of feline brothel. At times, his piggy little eyes light up and I half believe I can see a smile on the other side of his face.

Thinking of Peregrine's happy life I have avoided contributing to a charity that promotes the wholesale spaying of cats. One of my local health shops is big on petitions and collecting tins. I didn't mind signing against blood sports, or dog-eating in Korea, or for them to have a license to sell organic wines, but spaying is another thing altogether. There's a lot of self-righteousness involved in the way pets are kept. Bourgeois owners must take away their sexuality and then, later, their life when they become inconveniently ill. I do not intend to do either to Peregrine.

Edwina Currie for a while played the good neighbour and tried to alter everyone's lives. In an act halfway between Marie Antoinette's 'Let them eat cake' and the do-gooding kids in Sunday School-prize novels she told the pensioners to knit themselves woolly hats and wear silk long johns. The old devils kept on dying of hypothermia as if to spite her. Then she went to work on eggs. There's something about propaganda that always makes me want to go and do the opposite. Since she spoke out I have been enjoying myself with piperades, four-egg omelettes and runny boiled eggs with soldiers. The Grinner's very partial to a nice bit of salmonella off my plate.

Adverts don't really need to be favourable. Edwina's words simply reminded me how good eggs were. Now the Government is spending money on TV ads to tell us to look after our hearts. An averagely puffy man is seen stuffing his face. Eventually his young daughter appears with a sketch of Mummy and Daddy, showing him as a big fat blob. We are left with the look of dawning recognition on his face. In reality, unless she'd had her hand held by Mummy, young Miss Clever Clogs would have drawn both her parents as blobs. Children usually do. Both my parents were blobs.

Poethons and Sex Talk

I have been labelled many things: 'the best-looking poet since Rupert Brooke' (Laurie Lee); 'a bit like Edna Everage' to perform after (Sir Stephen Spender); and Byron's twentieth-century heir. To top it all, I am now 'the thinking woman's crumpet' or rather part of it, thanks to Sophia Fraser, the organiser of the Poethon, a marathon reading by poets. In publicising the event she told journalists that all the thinking woman's crumpet would be assembled to read – no mention of the thinking man's crumpet. I have always known, of course, that I don't appeal to thinking men. It's probably just as well – most of them think so much that they never get down to sex. The Poethon was in aid of buying a property in Moniack Mhor, near Inverness, to start something analogous to writers' Arvon courses. A leaflet pinned to the noticeboard told us that Moniack Mhor means either 'my great lady' or 'big bog', which seems to imply that 'bog' and 'lady' are synonymous in Gaelic.

When Moniack Mhor gets going, I expect some of the thinking woman's crumpet will be invited to be tutors on study weekends. Most of them already teach Arvon courses. The thinking woman's crumpet, I am told, send in their oldest photo for the publicity leaflet, then turn up with a new haircut and tight jeans, hoping. . . .

Poets are odd creatures. Sophia Fraser's thank-you letter to us reveals the world's opinion: 'I imagine a poet's is a very private mind and probably much happier crouching behind a book when subjected to the public in performance.' Apparently what the audience enjoyed most was seeing us without our shields (we'd had to memorise our stuff). 'It was like watching children talking to the camera. There is no sophistication.' Thanks, Sophia.

Personally, I've always been more of a flasher than a croucher, poetically speaking. I enjoy the performing bit even if

I don't go about it in tight jeans, hoping to be taken for the thinking woman's crumpet. My flasher mentality got me on the controversial Channel Four chat show *Sex Talk* later the same month. I'm convinced from some of the calls that I get that I'm in every researcher's Filofax under 'Sex'. (If not, boys and girls, please make a note of it.)

The panel for a discussion or chat show is carefully picked first. Researchers make long phone calls to you or meet you for lunch. By the time you're on the air, everyone has a pretty good idea what you are going to say on the subject. There's the token writer (me), the experts and the members of the public (often embryo actors). The sole qualification is that you have to be prepared to talk openly and honestly about the secret areas of your life, or at least put on a fair imitation of doing so. If you don't have the opinion expected of you when the researchers ring up, you won't get the job. This happened to me with the *After Dark* show. The researcher seemed to want me to be ready to slaughter Shere Hite verbally on air. I felt he almost wanted a guarantee. I pointed out that as I hadn't met her or read her books, I could only respond to whatever she had to say. Not good enough – I wasn't hired. It would be fun, one day, to be involved in a real cat-fight on TV. I don't know about Shere Hite, but I would love either Barbara Cartland or Mrs White-house as a sparring partner.

The *Sex Talk* group's opinions weren't different enough for a good fight. Six of us were discussing the merits of sex and celibacy. But, curiously, the longest-serving celibates and the non-celibates were not so far apart. I don't know what will end up on the cutting-room floor, but one of the questions that arose was what we hoped for in the nineties. I said a cure for AIDS because of the threat hanging over friends and myself. Now, not being the sensitive, frailer kind of poet, I would have to say that I'm horribly healthy – touch wood. I've not contracted a cold or a cough, let alone HIV, this year. It just seemed less self-righteous to include myself. There, but for the grace of condoms, go I. . . .

After filming we adjourned to a hotel for cakes and coffee.

We had got on well, so there were hugs and kisses all round as we said our goodbyes – except for Kev, the Welsh hairdresser. 'Don't kiss me on the lips, dear!' he muttered nervously as he lunged for my forehead and nose, although he'd had his leg pressed against mine throughout the filming. Could it possibly have been my remark about AIDS towards the end? Hadn't his mum told him you catch things from lavatory seats, not girls' mouths?

Pensioners and Poetry Editors

I have just received an angry letter from a member of the Normandy Veterans Association because I wrote in a previous column that I didn't fancy the thought of a 75-year-old called Chuck descending on me. 'Who the heck do you think is going to fancy you when you are seventy-five?' the irate veteran wants to know. Nobody, of course. I am saving every pound I earn for a toy-boy-cum-chauffeur-cum-masseur to tell me a few lies when I grow old. I realise it will not be cheap. Unlike Chuck, I shall avoid sending my c.v. to a known writer less than half my age with a note, 'Is she your kinda gal?' Nor will Mr Urwin of the Normandy Veterans be getting the apology he demands. The fact that he and Chuck and all the others fought in the last war does not entitle any of them to free sex and/or hospitality with someone born long after that war. They should stay in their league and chat up some old dear in the pension queue – she might even be grateful if she hasn't saved enough to afford a toy-boy.

At a recent dinner party, I was told by Michael Longley that Irish poets, especially the outspoken ones, receive regular death threats. It seems poets and poetry are taken more seriously in Ireland. Mercifully, I have never received a death threat – not even a rape threat. People assume that I'm only too willing to oblige. This month an article of mine, 'Gentlemen Callers', appeared in *Forum*. I theorised that obscene phone callers were no worse than double-glazing salesmen and, though a nuisance, could be amusing at times. Immediately I received a letter from a lecturer, who asked me very respectfully when could he make his obscene call and what subject would I like it on. On the same day the article appeared, feeling a great hypocrite, I trotted off to my local police station to report my most persistent caller. Someone who phones once can be funny, but Lee had clocked up about a hundred calls over the last two years – sometimes five in one day – and had also been foolish enough to give me his name and address. Of course, Lee hasn't taken a blind bit of notice of the Colchester police, any more than he has of my telling him he's an insane creep and I'm not interested in his body. I had been threatening him with the police for weeks beforehand. He didn't mind the thought of them coming to see him, but begged me, 'Please don't tell them I've got a short cock!' Being kind at heart I spared him that humiliation. After all, the sergeant concerned had enough of a job keeping a straight face when I said that Lee had been demanding a pair of my panties to wear. Lee now tells me that he showed my books to the police and told them I loved all men as his excuse. I've often described my promiscuity as phil-anthropy, but I'm afraid this doesn't extend as far as crazy phone callers (or septuagenarians). Still, I suppose Lee's given me some good publicity. I don't imagine the boys in blue of Colchester would have thought of looking at my books but for him.

The other life-enhancer this month has been having one of my poems vetoed by Craig Raine, the poetry editor of Faber and Faber. John Whitworth, the poet who had selected my work for an anthology, embarrassed at having his choice overruled, wrote me an apologetic letter. Now, if this anthology had been targeted at primary schools I might well have understood – but no, it was a collection of *blue* verse. Can my poem have offended Mr Raine's delicate sensibilities? Unlikely, considering that one of his own best-known verses is entitled 'Arsehole'. It would be wrong, of course, for me to assume that his editorial interference sprang from misogyny. The work of the academic, translator and poet John Adlard also got the chop. In reply to his letter to me on the subject, I wrote a simple card, saying that I too was excluded: 'My "Big Pricks" got up Craig Raine's nose, alas – but I'll see he gets his come-uppance.'

Beastly Behaviour

The unusual crime of bestiality always excites the curiosity of humans, sometimes their feelings too. During the war years, an innocent friend of my mother's was grabbed by a young policeman when she asked him to explain what it was while she was idling a morning away at the Old Bailey. While I can see the attraction of Jersey cows for farm-workers (those lovely long eyelashes), I have always been puzzled and a little fascinated by the case of the man who was arrested for doing it with a puffin. I would love to know why and, more importantly, how.

Bestiality has from time to time been the subject of literature from the Greek myths on. The Greeks recognised this interesting phenomenon: not only did peasants enjoy putting sheep's legs down their wellies (or rather, goats' legs lashed to sandals in those days), but the practice was also found in more up-market versions like Pasiphae and the bull (the result being the Minotaur). It was also seen that animals could, in their turn, fancy men and women.

I've always been liked by animals in a more Platonic sort of way: moggies, Rottweilers, goats – you name it. But recently I encountered a hedgehog with an extraordinary passion for me – so much so that, for several weeks, he crashed in every night through a cat-door above a lavatory, made his way to my bedside and tugged at the bedding hopefully. It was a doomed passion, of course. He was well-endowed for a hedgehog, but hardly human size at an inch and a quarter. Besides, there were the prickles. . . . As the old joke goes, 'How do hedgehogs make love? Answer: Very, very carefully!'

It all started when I rescued him from a watery death with the aid of a walking stick. I had come in late after a posh magazine launch party and went to use the basement lavatory. Just as I was lowering my bum I heard squeaks and saw black eyes and a heaving mass of spines. My first reaction was to swear I'd never touch champagne again, but then I realised there *really was* something down there. Since then, my nightly visitant and I have become the best of friends; several hundred years ago I suppose we'd have been burned as witch and familiar. I thought about calling him Apollinaire – a pretentious joke as the French poet wrote a book of which the title can be loosely translated as *The 11,000 Pricks*. Instead I settled on Houdini, as he had escaped a watery death.

Aside from bestiality, humans have always been interested in animal sex, from the birds and the bees upwards. One of the chief attractions of nature programmes on telly is to find out how little-known species do it and what sort of lovers and/or parents they make. My own view is that judgements arrived at are really only generalisations. Tom cats are *supposed* to be poor lovers, but my Peregrine Pickle is a perfect gentleman.

Recently, I went round Jersey Zoo, which was started by Gerald Durrell. It's a zoo that specialises in conserving and breeding endangered species. It's almost the equivalent of a honeymoon hotel in the extent to which its workforce pimp for the animals and cater for their special needs. Naturally, almost all the species are there in twos. Visitors get quite sentimental about it. I heard one pitying the rhinoceros-iguana until his absurdly ugly mate waddled out of hiding: 'Ah! It's all right, he's got somebody!'

The males and females of species that don't let it all hang out can be difficult to tell apart. Parrots are so secretive about their private parts that their sex can only be ascertained with a probe while the bird is under anaesthetic. Remind me not to be a parrot in my next incarnation.

The gorilla pit is one of the zoo's chief attractions. The male gorilla, unlike most of the other males in the zoo, has only a small harem. He has proved such a virile chap in the past that the zoo's vet tranquillised him and performed certain intimate tests to find out his secret. Although the only thing the gorilla saw was the vet plus tranquilliser-gun (he was put back in his pit while still unconscious), he has never forgiven him and throws things or bellows whenever the man passes. 'Maybe he thought you had his wives while he was out for the count,' I suggested.

Like most of the visitors, I soon found myself looking for exhibitionistic animals prepared to do it in public. The fruit bats were perhaps involved in a 69, but it was hard to be sure in their darkened surroundings. Why, too, were there three tortoises in a cage? I postulated to the guide that it might be a *ménage à trois*. 'Ah, yes, the tortoises,' she said. 'We don't talk about them!' Then there were the Celebes apes. . . . They have nasty bare pink bottoms you can spot from 200 yards away. A notice explained: 'The pink bottoms have tough insensitive skin which enables the monkeys to sit still for long periods without fidgeting. This could be important when sleeping high in the trees.' Soon, two of them started a brief bout of sexual intercourse, or so I thought until I read the second notice: 'Sex does not play a dominant role in the behaviour of these monkeys. Some animals may be seen apparently mating. This may be a submissive gesture on the part of one of them.' Reminds me of a lot of humans I know.

Something Borrowed, Something Blue . . .

Every Christmas my mother, who's in her seventies, hears about a few more dead friends. Old school chums write to tell her who's gone when they send the annual Christmas card. 'Yes, I dreamed about so-and-so!' she says portentously. I've told her never to dream about me. At my time of life, it's less common to hear of friends dying, but if your friends come from as wide an age group as mine do, it's always a possibility.

Shortly before Christmas I heard of the death of Eric Parrott in a letter from his wife Tricia. I think I'd have felt sad even if I hadn't known and liked him. Over the last few years Eric Parrott edited a series of light-verse anthologies, send-ups of literature, history and opera, the most recent of these being *How to Be Well-Versed in Poetry*, a delightful skit on English poetry with verses on form, poems on poets and mini versions of long lyrics or epics, tailor-made for the lazy reader. Most of his contributors, myself included, came up from the ranks of the literary compers who win with clerihews, limericks and pastiche in the back pages of *The Spectator* and the *New Statesman*. Every year we used to have a mass get-together over lunch in a pub in Marylebone. Eric, who looked a little like Leo McKern, masterminded the whole operation, sending out frequent bulletins during the year, dragooning the laziest of us writers into producing something for the anthologies. The lunch was a time for swapping ideas for new books. Stupidly, I envisaged these pleasant annual meetings going on for ever. Eric's sight was failing, I knew, but his mind was so lively it was hard to think of him not being around for twenty more anthologies at least.

Eric was himself a good light-verse and pastiche poet. Quite how prolific he was will probably never be known. Perhaps in order to win more prizes in the *New Statesman* comps, he invented a whole series of names to write under with special personas to go with them. The majority of these names he would not own up to, although I did find out about Maud Gracechurch (a rather liberated Anglican spinster) and Wayne Sidesaddle. ('He's *real* dirty!') Eric's own persona was not always real clean, come to think of it. A fair proportion of his verses (often his funniest ones) were in the bawdy category, an honourable tradition in which English versifiers have excelled ever since Chaucer. There was the poem he penned for the *New Statesman* on Prince Charles and Princess Di's wedding night, written in imitation of my style. I never actually saw it, but the adjudicator claimed it was too filthy for that fairly liberal weekly to print.

Perhaps Eric's talent was the secret of his happy family life on a Dutch barge on the Regent's Canal. There's nothing like smutty rhymes for making a marriage work. Marriage-guidance councillors ought to recommend them as a hobby to their clients. My parents had great fun while my dad was alive, capping each other's rhymes in bed. He invented a form I like to call 'dirty triads' – unlike the majority of Welsh triads they were not on high-minded themes. They evolved out of his male desire to get the last word, or rather the last line, on any subject.

My father was part Scottish, which may have had a lot to do with it. The Scots, perhaps even more than the English, have often produced good bawdy writers. At the same time, the half of the nation that's not making filthy jokes is desperately concerned with keeping the sabbath and, worse still, keeping other people's morals in check. Robert Burns sent these types up admirably. They still exist.

Jesus had the right idea, associating with publicans and sinners and spurning the Pharisees. He'd have liked Amsterdam. On a recent visit to Holland I found that Dutch humour was bawdy and remarkably like ours. Unlike the English, the Dutch are also extremely urbane about morality. Perhaps the fact that a great many of them trained as artists is one reason for this. Art schools tend to breed a liberal temperament.

Amsterdam has been for years a place where gay men and women can express affection openly and where almost anything goes. Where else would a newspaper journalist admit to his interviewee (me) that his hobby was collecting vibrators? The Dutch are equally liberal about censorship. For once, I didn't have to worry about using four-letter words on television. The host of the afternoon literary chat show I was on said them first. Journalists I talked to there were staggered at my tale of how I'd phoned an editor on *The Independent* to ask if I could write 'willy' in a piece on strippergrams when quoting someone else's words. My editor said, 'Fine, put it in. . . .' I did, but it was taken out when the article was printed. Censorship of that kind simply does not exist in Dutch newspapers. If only civilised Amsterdam were warmer and had a few hills. I'd move there like a shot!

Educating Nigel

Educating Nigel

A good-looking couple are lying in an antique double bed. There are enough pillows to prop them up slightly so that their arms are above the sheets. They are lying close together but not touching. He is about forty-five and she is thirty. There are lamps (lit) on either side, standing on bedside cabinets. There is also a small pile of glossy magazines on the woman's side.

HELEN: So you think you're a new man because your wife makes you push the vacuum cleaner round?

NIGEL: You make me sound like a wimp.

HELEN: I'm sorry – I only meant to say that being a new man involves more than just doing 10, or even 50 per cent of the housework.

NIGEL: I reckon I do the lot – well, some weeks. Anyway, what do *you* think makes a 'new man'?

HELEN: I'm not absolutely sure, because I've certainly never met the animal. I only know what I'd *want* him to be like.

NIGEL: But women are women and men are men. It's all very well for you feminists to argue we're the same – don't think I haven't heard it all before – but it's simply not true. There's a lot of common sense to the old values. That's why they've kept going for centuries. They may sound objectionable, logically speaking – but they work.

HELEN: They don't work for me. I'm sick of prejudice on the job front.

NIGEL: But you've done all right for yourself – in the end. Women have got other methods. There's prejudice against men too. It wouldn't help me to get anything published if I went to see someone in a short skirt.

65

HELEN: Oh, I don't know . . . I can think of one particular editor who might be tempted.

NIGEL: I'm serious. Editors have *got* to be cautious about using women writers in case they go off to have babies and expect sick leave. You don't catch us men having a year's sabbatical on full pay for one of those.

HELEN: What's this 'full pay' and 'sick leave'? We get advances for books, we freelance – we're self-employed, in other words. Neither of us has any chance of sabbaticals, however pregnant we get.

NIGEL: I was just making a general point. Anyway, it makes sense to stick to the old values. Men have to be paid more so that they can ask girls out, or bring up a family once somebody's pinned them down. It takes a lot of cash these days.

HELEN: I'd rather pay my own way. It's not only money, though. We want the same rights sexually.

NIGEL: But we're *not* the same. Haven't you heard the saying 'A standing cock knows no conscience'?

HELEN: I hadn't.

NIGEL: It just means that we're always ready for a bit of the other – horny . . . randy . . . you know.

HELEN: Randy? You? What a bloody joke! You're lying next to a woman with only a thin bit of blue satin on her. You fancy her and she's fifteen years younger than you. What more do you want?

NIGEL: You're not as young as Carol.

HELEN: And soon you'll find Carol's not as young as somebody else. If you need younger and younger girls to get it up, the logical conclusion of that is you'll end up being arrested for putting your fingers up some baby's nappy.

NIGEL: No thanks! You can keep babies.

HELEN: There's this absurd idea that men have about being seen with a woman a generation or two younger. They actually think it makes *them* look younger. The reverse is true.

NIGEL: Come off it! Everybody admires film stars for doing it. A beautiful young woman's the ultimate status symbol – like owning a Porsche.

HELEN: Owning! Who *owns* women? The slave trade's been abolished. Hadn't you heard? No, I still maintain that men who go out with very young girls just make themselves look old. I'll show you what I mean. My father used to enjoy taking trips with me when I was all tarted up at sixteen or so. Now, he was in his mid-forties when I was born, so there was a good age gap between us. Then, one day, when we were out together, some tactless bus conductor asked how old my 'grandad' was. Yes . . . that shattered the romance of it all for him. He wasn't so keen on being seen with me after that. It would have been even worse, of course, if I'd been some bimbo he'd picked up and was spending money on. Daughters come cheaper.

NIGEL: Yes, but you say there was a huge age gap between you and your father – also, judging by that picture on your desk, he'd really let himself go. I jog and work out. I'll never be a pound over what I should be. No, you can't beat the feeling of pulling someone young. I see the sixth-formers from the local comprehensive looking interested when I'm out in my new tracksuit. It matches my eyes.

HELEN: Who's a pretty boy then? I wasn't talking about you. I was thinking of older men. It may feel great to them, pulling someone young, but it doesn't make them *look* great. That's what I'm getting at. You see some really ill-assorted couples in the papers. Comedians and game-

show hosts seem particularly prone to marrying the
dancers on their shows. In fact, they do it regularly. You
see the same bloke, every year or two, getting more and
more wrinkled, saying, 'This time it's love!' Samantha or
Susie sits by his side and goes along with it all. Then, a year
or two on, you hear about the expensive divorce. Those
men don't look young – *women* all see them as old fools. I
don't wish to say that somewhere, some time, there can't
be genuine affection between those of different generations
– but 99.9 per cent of the time you can rely on the whole
thing being a rip-off.

NIGEL: But it takes a real man to pull a young girl. My friend
John, he's very virile, and he's not a game-show host. He
brings girls back to the office – screws them against the
filing-cabinets. He's sixty-odd.

HELEN: Says he screws them, more like. How old are these
girls?

NIGEL: Oh, the age girls are gorgeous at – seventeen or so –
mid-twenties at worst.

HELEN: (*laughs*): Young enough to be his granddaughter?

NIGEL: He can still pull them.

HELEN: Is he rich?

NIGEL: Well, yes.

HELEN: Silly old bugger. I expect he thinks it's love. He'll probably finish himself off.

NIGEL: He's had five heart attacks.

HELEN: They always do.

NIGEL: Power's an aphrodisiac. Women like older men.

HELEN: No, *money's* an aphrodisiac. Older men without money
are called dirty old men if they try anything on.

NIGEL: Is that what you think I am?

HELEN: No, you're not quite old enough. You'll have to wait another fifteen or twenty years before becoming a dirty old man. Anyway, I'm not young enough to be a bimbo, either. You had some sense picking someone nearer your age. With me by your side, you might well pass for ten or fifteen years younger – in a bad light. (*She laughs.*)

NIGEL: If I were rich you'd fancy me.

HELEN: But I *do* fancy you. Why else am I lying here beside you? Why else did I make dinner so late that you missed your train and had to stay the night? Why else did I go out and buy two bottles of wine – which is something I hardly touch under normal circumstances? Why else did I tell you the spare bed was damp and haunted? Can't you be randy enough to take what's on offer and be grateful?

NIGEL: You make too many decisions. You've done all this on purpose. It's too obvious. A real man likes to think of these things for himself. That's what I mean when I talk about the old values. There's a right way and a wrong way of going about things.

HELEN: That's a bit conventional.

NIGEL: I'm not ashamed of it. Women like flowers – I give the odd bouquet. I open doors. You all like that sort of attention.

HELEN: Do you think we wouldn't trade the whole lot in for complete equality? You say 'a real man' likes to think of things for himself. Everybody likes that. In any case, what's your definition of a *real* man? Do you know any? Which of your friends come into that category? And no, I don't mean I want an introduction. I've had enough of *real* men for tonight.

NIGEL: It's like that magazine said. (*He gestures towards the bedside table.*) Men are randy devils.

HELEN: Huh!

NIGEL: It's true. Men have to have affairs. One woman's never enough for them. Being at home with the kids is enough, though, for a woman.

HELEN: Well, what if she hasn't got kids?

NIGEL: She's belly-aching about wanting the damn things then and blaming a poor chap for having a low sperm count. What does he need a high count for? It only takes one sperm – holed in one, as they say in golf. A high count might even be a disadvantage – the little beggars might knock each other down in the race.

HELEN: Fair enough. Actually, though, I think it's meant to be a bit like owning a lot of premium bonds – ups the chances of winning, if pregnancy can be counted as winning. Anyway, I'm not blaming you for having a low sperm count, if that's your problem. I'm only interested in my career and my affairs. I'm a bit like those real men you keep talking about.

NIGEL: I know it's all talk with you. Women don't do that kind of thing. Anyway, I was telling you which men I admired, wasn't I? Well, there's my friend Mike – known him since school. He's very well-read – a cultured bloke. I sometimes go to him for advice about my novels when I'm going through a sticky patch. He can always recognise somebody else's plot. He's a great one for the women – at least he used to be before he went and shacked up with his wife again. She must be nearly as old as he is – bit of a bloody come-down. He used to pick up girls – two at a time. He could handle it. He liked two. He was a real man, all right. He could drink anyone I knew under the table. We used to sink a bottle of tequila together and then he'd say, 'How about a whisky chaser?' and bring out a flask from his back pocket. Great bloke! Great drinker.

HELEN: You talk as if he were dead.

NIGEL: Well, he might as well be. Dead from the waist down, that's what his wife's made him. He never tells me anything about his sex life these days.

HELEN: And I suppose Mike was never made to miss his train by a girl?

NIGEL: Good God, no! He never allowed himself to be caught in any way. He once even shinned down a drainpipe when he saw this tart's husband coming back.

HELEN: Tarts? Oh, I see now. I thought you said he could pull any woman. Men who go to tarts can't pull anybody. Why else would they pay for sex?

NIGEL: That's not true. Some people like an exact bargain. You can pay all down the line and get nothing with a lot of good girls.

HELEN: You don't have to pay all down the line with me. I buy my round just like one of the lads.

NIGEL: That's the trouble. You're too much like one of the lads. *Vive la différence!* It's no fun without it, in fact. I like to pay for women – but not too much.

HELEN: You're just mean.

NIGEL: I know. If I wasn't mean I'd have paid for a hotel room when I missed my train. Anyway, you're mean too – you expect me to do things for my night's lodging. I can see that smug suffering look on your face. 'I've fed him; I've given him a bed for the night; now I'm lying back waiting for my multiple orgasm.' You women have got twice as bad about wanting things like that since *Cosmopolitan* and all the other glossies got going. Nobody cared about multiple orgasms when they read *Woman's Realm*.

HELEN (*laughing*): I think I'd be prepared to settle for a simple orgasm. I've never been entirely sure what multiple ones are. Anyway, I don't expect a thing from you now – not even half an orgasm. Admittedly, when I first planned this. . . . I mean – any other man would!

NIGEL: That's another example of inequality. Men are always expected to perform. That's what ruins sex for us. You plan and you wait for us like spiders or praying mantises. You're worse than most. It's spoiled everything tonight – the planning. I had thought I'd linger on after dinner, then ask to use your spare bed, then meander into your room once you'd had time to undress. But no, you had to say that bed was haunted. Haunted, my arse. That was obvious. What's it haunted by – the ghosts of men you've shagged out? I don't like women who are on the Pill, either. You've even got the bloody things laid out on that cut-glass tray on your dressing table – like trophies.

HELEN: That's only so I can remember to take them when I put my make-up on in the morning.

NIGEL: That's what I mean – calculating. You're worse than any other woman I know. Womanly women at least forget sometimes. They don't take the damn things like clockwork. I bet you never forget.

HELEN: Why should I want to forget? Nobody forgets to take the Pill unless they do so deliberately. Can't you see through that sort of woman? Women decide they can't mix children and a career – or else they've had as many kids as they want and that's why they take it. There's no reason for us to forget – we've got too much to lose. How many of us can afford kids and a mortgage these days? No, I've heard of cases of women 'forgetting' it. They do that when they want to trap some dumb bastard. It's pretty soon a phantom pregnancy when the bloke refuses to marry her; or sometimes even when he agrees – always after, not before, though. If some girl tries that one with you, make sure she's pregnant and, later, make sure the child's yours. They can do tests now. Anyway, what am I telling you for? You don't want a woman on the Pill.

NIGEL: Too right. The man should provide the contraception. I could have gone to some late-night chemist's. It's more fun that way, even if they've run out and you have to risk things. It's very unwomanly going on the Pill unless a man's told you to. Did you go on it for someone?

HELEN: Only for myself. Like most women, I know men can't be trusted with contraception. God help us if they invent pills for men.

NIGEL: I'd be perfectly capable of taking a pill as long as I had a nice hot drink to wash it down.

HELEN: Yes, and we all know who'd have to make the drink.

NIGEL (*laughs*): You wouldn't begrudge me a cup of coffee now, would you?

HELEN: No. You can have a cup, or a pot if you like. We don't seem to have anything better to do. Perhaps you'd rather have cocoa? That's supposed to be aphrodisiac.

NIGEL: You talk too much. Don't you realise that talk's the enemy of performance? You're as much to blame as I am.

HELEN: OK, I'll stop.

HELEN *moves away from* NIGEL *and lies back. There is silence for a minute.* HELEN *looks across at* NIGEL *and opens her mouth as if to speak. He looks at her then starts to laugh.*

NIGEL: It's going to be a long night. I suppose we might as well talk.

HELEN: I hope you've got some private detective spying on us for your divorce petition. I feel as if I'm in an old film – I'm the chambermaid and you're the toff who's paying me. Perhaps we ought to play gin rummy.

NIGEL: You know I'd never get divorced. I don't want to lose my home. That bitch never put a penny into it – she even gets me to go and have keys cut for her lovers. She's made my place feel less like home than an office or a public urinal and yet the law would say she's entitled to half. That's inequality.

HELEN (*angrily, rising to a crescendo*): Look, let's not talk about your wife again. I know she's a prize cow, but staying with her was your choice. I've had enough of all those complaints. In fact, I reckon you owe me about five thousand pounds in psychotherapy fees for all the counselling I've given you over this. If you're fed up with her, get shut or shut up. Anything else makes you ridiculous. You say she's unfaithful. Well, do the same back. Or don't. Stop shilly-shallying. I could stand you being faithful to her if only you didn't pretend to be the other thing. If you're too moral for adultery, fine – admit it.

NIGEL: I'm not. Ours is an open marriage. I'm a modern enough man for that. My wife doesn't do half she claims, of course. She's just trying to make me jealous, poor old thing. Women have to do things like that once their looks have faded.

HELEN: But you said she had lovers?

NIGEL: She's too frigid. She just likes to flirt.

HELEN: She needs spare door keys to flirt?

NIGEL: Well . . . I really *do* play around. I've given the odd key away too. Things are different for men. We're randy devils. I like to play the field.

HELEN: That's one name for it. Which field? A football field with the other lads?

NIGEL: Helps keep me in shape. Then there's always the pub after a game. Men are better company than women. You know where you are with a man.

HELEN (*mutters*): I don't – not with you. (*Out loud.*) Well, who do you play the other sort of field with? Certainly not me. You only talk about playing it with me.

NIGEL: There's Sarah and Carol and Kate and there were those two Vietnamese nurses.

HELEN: And all the other names in your address book. Yes, I have noticed – you always flash them ostentatiously under my nose when you're making dates with me. It's easy enough to get people's numbers at parties, isn't it? I've got lists of numbers too. I hardly remember who half of them belong to. Oh, I don't doubt you've been out with those girls – like you have with me. But do you, can you, follow through? How many beds have you lain in doing nothing, just like this? One of these days I'm going to take down all those numbers and throw a party and invite Sarah and Carol and Kate and the Vietnamese nurses, and all the others. There won't be any men. We'll just compare notes.

NIGEL: Bloody lesbian!

HELEN: This is the first time I've ever been to bed with a man who's called me that. If you were gay we could have been good friends. I've had plenty of gay friends – but then, we didn't end up in bed together. You call yourself randy – you're as randy as Abelard after he'd had his operation. Did the Vietnamese nurses cut it off or something?

NIGEL: Don't be silly – they were great.

HELEN: Yes, great, fab and all the rest. Are you sure they weren't groovy too? Those words date you. We're *all* human beings, don't you realise that? When you bring out some arguments, I can respect you – even if they're wrong-minded ones – but this talk of things being 'great' . . . honestly! It sounds unbelievably naïve. If I hadn't overheard other men drivelling on about their conquests in the same vein, I'd think you were talking down to me deliberately. You're a highly intelligent man on the subject of literature, art, theatre – almost anything but women. When it comes to them, all you can think of is adjectives like 'great'.

NIGEL: How about gorgeous, nubile, willing (*pauses to think for a moment*) . . . nympho?

HELEN: Typical. What have you been doing – reading the ads in the *Sunday Sport*? I reckon you're living in fantasy-land. Perhaps you're still a virgin – well, near enough: shop-soiled, but not really experienced. You remind me of this poet I know. She has readings in London where only one or two people turn up – I know, I went to one. Then she gets a snippet into the *Brentford Gazette* saying what a wonderful reading, with hundreds in the audience, she had in Newcastle and how much better things are up North. I have this inkling that she goes to Newcastle and nobody turns up, then she writes a piece for the *Newcastle Chronicle* saying how much better things are in the South. It's amazing how you can keep an illusion going. It's like juggling – keeping all your balls in the air while being terrified the whole thing's going to come crashing down round your ears. I suppose I represent the West and the Vietnamese nurses are the East in your piece of prestidigitation?

NIGEL: The Vietnamese nurses told me I was great too.

HELEN: I suppose it was the only word of English they knew. Some witty shit had probably told them it meant 'bastard'.

NIGEL: I *am* a great lover. Sarah and Carol and Kate told me so as well.

HELEN: If I tell you you're a great lover will you be one?

HELEN *pauses and looks across at him.* NIGEL *looks away.*

HELEN: No, I'm not going to say it until there's a reason for it. You'd only go and tell Sarah and Carol and Kate.

NIGEL: And the two Vietnamese nurses. . . .

HELEN: And the two Vietnamese nurses, while you lay in bed with them doing *nothing*. I bet your friend Mike's as bad. You men stick together like Freemasons or something.

NIGEL: Did I tell you about the other two nurses who took me home when I was in Edinburgh?

HELEN (*sighs*): You did.

NIGEL: I prefer air hostesses, though – they're more cosmopolitan.

HELEN: Like this? (*She picks up a magazine and taps the cover.*)

NIGEL: No, not that feminist twaddle. I mean they've seen a thing or two.

HELEN: Did they see yours, then? That's more than I've done. You got into bed with your boxer shorts on – very unhygienic, I thought. What am I supposed to do to turn you on – dress up in a uniform?

NIGEL: It might help.

HELEN *gets out of bed, rummages in a case on the floor and finds something. She holds up a crumpled nurse's uniform.*

HELEN: Here, look at this. I got it in Oxfam for a pound. I've seamed it in – it's a perfect fit now. Shall I try it on? (*She starts to lift up her long blue nightdress slowly, as if she's going to take it off.*)

NIGEL: No, stop. You'll catch cold. Don't be silly. Get back into bed.

HELEN *drops the nurse's uniform on top of the case, gives* NIGEL *a mock salute and gets back in.*

HELEN: Ah, he wants me in bed with him.

HELEN *moves across as if to snuggle up to* NIGEL. NIGEL *stays put, neither accepting nor rejecting her head on his shoulder.*

HELEN (*shivers*): I really am cold.

NIGEL: Serves you right for getting out to put on that silly nurse's uniform.

HELEN: You don't think they're silly when somebody else wears them. I can't do a thing right. You once said I wasn't a very 'womanly' woman. How much more womanly do you want? I've sympathised with you about your wife. I've cooked for you and given you plonk and made you miss your last train. I'm lying in bed next to you and you don't even want to touch me.

NIGEL: So you keep telling me. Men don't want to be nagged.

HELEN: But some of them *need* it. So – I nag. Isn't that a woman-ly quality? You talk of 'womanly' and you talk of girls. Wouldn't it be better to say girlish?

NIGEL: I know what I mean. I only fancy girls – women are too old. But womanliness is a quality you all should have.

HELEN: OK – let's define your perfect woman. Do you want a bimbo on the outside and a wife and mother lurking within?

NIGEL: I don't really go for bimbos.

HELEN: No, I forgot – a nurse or an air hostess.

NIGEL: They don't have to be that. They just need the right qualities. Youth and vulnerability so that I can feel protec-tive.

HELEN: I have never yet seen a vulnerable air hostess or nurse. The first are just over-made-up glorified waitresses. The others . . . vulnerable – you must be joking. They'd give you a vicious blanket bath with a scrubbing brush soon as look at you.

NIGEL: I don't think I'd mind that.

HELEN: OK, anything to please. I've only got a sauna brush,

though. It's a German one so it's fairly hard and military. Will that do?

HELEN *starts to get out of bed, but* NIGEL *puts his hand on her arm to stop her.*

NIGEL: Don't get out again, you'll make both of us cold.

HELEN: What else do you want from your perfect woman? Cordon bleu cookery? Wonderful sex? Money?

NIGEL: You don't understand. You haven't listened. Just think back to the things I said about tradition. Your system's like Communism – all very nice in theory, but it's collapsing now. Morality is not what any successful society's about. There's got to be a kind of capitalism between the sexes. The bosses dominate. The workers are given a little security in exchange. When they're too old they're retired.

HELEN (*mutters*): *Women* are never too old for it.

NIGEL (*goes on without noticing*): Capitalism's a system that has always worked and always will. Britain never has revolutions – change need only be gradual. I can stand a little feminism if it keeps a girl happy, as long as she doesn't try to upset the whole apple cart. Things run smoothly enough as they are. I just want an ordinary girl – nice and ordinary. Someone who'll show some gratitude for what I spend on her.

HELEN: But one who doesn't cost too much?

NIGEL: Yes.

HELEN: You've told me what you want from a woman. Now I shall tell you what I have to offer. Take it or leave it – this is what I am. If I go for a meal with you I want to pay my share. If you buy me a drink I want to buy you one back.

NIGEL: But what if I don't want a second drink?

HELEN: Fine, there's always another time. We earn much the

same – I should pay my way. And about work: I want you
to respect mine, my writing I mean, as much as I respect
yours. Now, when it comes to sex – if it ever comes to sex –
I would like to be able to say I fancy you and I want you
without being despised. Above all, I don't want to have to
tell any lies. I don't want to have to say no when I mean
yes, or vice versa. And I'd like to be able to take the
initiative – sometimes.

HELEN *turns towards* NIGEL *and leans across and kisses him linger-*
ingly on the lips, one hand brushing his cheek. Nigel just accepts it but
does nothing. HELEN *lies back.*

HELEN: This isn't going to work. Perhaps there's a man – new
or old – somewhere who'll accept me for what I am.

HELEN *puts out the light on her side and turns her back on* NIGEL,
snuggling down as if she's about to go to sleep. He turns slightly and
looks at her. HELEN *starts to talk again. Her voice is lighter now and*
more girlish for the rest of the conversation.

HELEN: Nigel, it's so lovely to have a man about the house. I get
so nervous on my own. (*She pauses.*) It's hard for a girl on
her own – so many little things we can't do. I get these
tension headaches and I can't reach the back of my neck to
massage it. In fact I think I'm getting a headache now.

NIGEL: Let me see if I can help.

NIGEL *moves across and puts one hand on* HELEN's *bare shoulder. He*
starts to massage both shoulders gently and begins kissing the back of
her neck.

HELEN: Oh, you're so good at it. It must be wonderful to have
such strong hands. My hands are so weak, I can't do
anything.

NIGEL: But you said you mended the roof?

HELEN: Did I? I meant I got a man in to do it. I hate dealing with workmen – a woman doesn't have the authority a man does.

NIGEL, *reassured, continues to kiss* HELEN *and gets closer, putting his arms round her and starting to feel her breasts.*

HELEN (*murmurs unconvincingly as* NIGEL's *upper arm moves down under the bedclothes*): Don't! Don't! Oh! I think I forgot the Pill this morning.

NIGEL: Don't worry, I'm a man of experience. I know how to stop a girl getting pregnant. Men learn these techniques from each other. I'd better put my light off first – I don't like to see what I'm doing.

The lights go down.

Letters to Hugo

Introduction

The letters on the following pages come from a long correspondence with the poet Hugo Williams. We were close friends
for six years, discounting a six-month hiatus in the middle.

We first met in late 1984 at the Poetry Society. I had just won
a small prize in the National Poetry Competition. After I'd gone
up to receive it, Hugo rushed across the room to me as if he'd
been stung, introduced himself and talked for half an hour or
so. He wrote afterwards, asking me to meet him for a drink.
That was the beginning of our friendship and correspondence.

I was attracted to him immediately, as I believe he was to me
– though he has since denied this. Over the next few months I
fell in love with him. At that stage he was nothing but kind and
considerate. After I'd known him a month or two, he started to
tell me intimate details about his marriage. I've never really
liked the idea of adultery, but in a few cases it seems justified.
Gradually, as I came to know Hugo better, I began to feel it was
almost my Christian duty. I sensed a chemistry between us and
soon came to realise that I would like nothing better than an
affair with him. I was in love, for the first time in my life.
Probably an element of pity for what he seemed to be suffering
at home entered into this.

Apart from the fact of Hugo's being married, there were other
things that separated us. At that stage I was still living with my
mother. That hadn't been a problem in my affairs with single men,
because they all had their own homes. But in Hugo's case, his
place was also his wife's. If there was to be an affair, something
would have to be arranged verbally. (I sometimes stayed at the
Chelsea Arts Club, which would have presented possibilities with
a different kind of man.) I was also afraid that Hugo might be
diffident about his age – he's nearly thirteen years older than me –
and might feel that he had nothing to offer me in the worldly
sense. As a freelance-cum-poet he was not well off.

Some people will say that if Hugo had wanted sex, he'd have got down to it earlier. I might have said the same if I hadn't had a similar experience with another half-Welsh man of the surname Williams. (He's subsequently changed his name, thinking 'Williams' too common for the acting profession.) We were both working as theatre ushers at the time, and we went round together: the odd trip to the cinema on our nights off, or drinks after work – that sort of thing. He treated me as a friend, not seeming to want to go any further. I stopped seeing him. About eighteen months later, he had nine gins at a party and wanted nothing more than to go back to my place. We had sex, although by that time, as he'd kept me waiting so long, I had rather gone off him. That experience told me some men might secretly want me, but be incapable of expressing that need for months or years. I put Hugo into this same category of low-libidoed, mixed-up Brits. I began to believe that I would have to be the one to initiate an affair.

About two years into our friendship, in January 1987, Hugo and I were having coffee in a bar in Islington. It was there that I risked making my verbal pass – I'd done no more than flirt before. Hugo was absolutely horrified, behaving like a straight man who's been groped by a particularly repulsive homosexual, or a shocked priest repelling an elderly nymphomaniac parishioner. He was so nasty he reduced me to tears, saying amongst other things that he only used to ask me out because I left pauses in our conversations on the telephone. I rang him two weeks later (perhaps unwisely). I hoped he'd apologise and blame his behaviour on problems at home – he always seemed to have those. Instead, he told me he 'despised me thoroughly' and never wanted to hear my 'stupid voice again'. I ran into him once or twice after that at literary parties and he behaved as if nothing had happened.

When Hugo rejected me so nastily, my first reaction was to go and write a satirical poem about him. I penned 'Just Good Friends' on the wings of rage and sent it to the *London Review of Books*. It was accepted by return and appeared in the very next edition – a swifter revenge than I could have possibly hoped for. I also took up weight-training with the secret purpose of getting strong enough to knock Hugo down publicly. Maybe I'll do it one day, if the circumstances are right.

About six months later, Hugo's wife got hold of my poem, which quotes some of the gems he said about her, and he found himself in a lot of trouble. He rang up, angrily reproaching me with 'spilling confidences'. I pointed out that I wouldn't have told on him if he hadn't dropped me in such a nasty way. Curiously, that poem was the catalyst in patching up our friendship. Hugo wrote me an abject letter, wanting me back. I said yes, of course, although I've often regretted my generosity in agreeing so easily.

Our letters became friendly again, but we did not meet as often as before and the friendship was punctuated with a series of petty acts. Presumably, Hugo never really forgave me for publishing 'Just Good Friends', or was it that he was jealous of my growing fame? At the end of 1990, I felt I had to call a halt to the friendship. By now, Hugo had told me he despised me a good many times. The acts of spite had become more and more frequent. To top it all he now said that he'd never fancied me and didn't consider me attractive in any way, even objectively speaking. No man could ever have taken any notice whatsoever of me, he insisted, or I wouldn't have over-estimated his interest in me and fallen in love with him. Curiously, the last time he phoned me, amid all the insults, be repeated that he was very fond of me, and that we would be friends in the future. We wouldn't, I told him, and made an end of it.

I'm not naturally a masochist, but I probably would have stood a sado-masochistic affair with Hugo because I loved him. A love–hate friendship is a complete impossibility, though. To quote the old Jewish joke, 'With friends like him, who needs enemies!' You need to be able to rely on the good will of your friends and I couldn't rely on that from Hugo any longer.

When I wrote them, I intended these letters to be purely between Hugo and myself. I kept copies, more for personal re-perusal than posterity. Looking back at them now, I believe that they were the truest things I've ever written. I haven't told any lies in my poems or in my travel book *Journeys to the Underworld*, but these letters are truer because they reveal *all* of myself – the tender side as well as the hard, cynical outsider. One of my greatest regrets at the ending of our friendship is that I'm denied this form of expression. My love affairs have been too short to involve letter-writing. I can be reasonably witty in letters to some friends, editors, my agent and so on – especially if these people have a good sense of humour themselves – but I'm denied the chance to put down on paper the full repertoire of emotions.

I hoped to charm Hugo and win his love and affection in this correspondence, but I failed miserably. In the end, he told me he found my letters 'dreary and boring'. It was those words that decided me to publish them. I have always been a believer in using everything in life – the bad and the good. In that spirit I give a selection of the most interesting of my Hugo letters to the world.

The following is the first of my long letters to Hugo. We had just had a drink together and he'd suggested I send him the manuscript of *Sky Ray Lolly*, which Andrew Motion of Chatto and Windus had rejected at that stage. Hugo offered to try it on his editor at the Oxford University Press.

23.1.85

Dear Hugo,

Sorry I misunderstood about the address – I think I only had the *New Statesman* one. I expect you thought I was really unreliable not getting the poems to you before your Oxford trip – I hope that went well for you, by the way.

Thanks for sending my stuff on to Will Sulkin. It's extremely kind of you to help like this. And thanks also for your comments on my work. I've sorted some of the poems that haven't been published – rather a large batch – but I wasn't too sure which type you'd like. I don't think I could be accused of lifting these ones from Larkin, anyway!*

I've been stuck in St Leonards the last week or two. We had about six inches of snow, storms, etc. Greedy as I am, I think I'd have stayed in and starved but for the cats. They kept standing by saucers staring reproachfully till I went out to lay in delicacies for them. The wretches have got too proud for tins and demand turkey legs from Hastings market. These are cheap enough, but large and cold and they tend to swing round and hit you on the shins or trip you up on the way home. Now the house is swimming due to burst pipes, slates off and the usual condensation, etc. I don't think there's any serious damage (yet), but it gets a little bit wearing moving books, clothes,

---

* When Hugo had published my poem 'The Goat Show' in the *New Statesman*, of which he is Poetry Editor, a month or two before we met, an angry Portuguese woman wrote in claiming I'd copied it from Philip Larkin's poem about a similar show. She made a number of line-by-line comparisons of a bizarre kind to try to prove her point. I didn't quite like to own up to Hugo that I had read very little Larkin, and certainly not the poem in question! Our first drink together was set up, ostensibly, so that he could show me her letter.

papers out of the way of each deluge, not to mention the mopping. (The mop's worn down to its last few hairs now!) It's lucky our carpets, etc. are so ancient that a few gallons more can't make any difference. (I suppose a nice, normal, bourgeois, non-sluttish set-up such as I have never known would show more damage.) The plumber's due today – I'll have the fun of fixing the slates. I'm dying for a hot bath. Being a bit of a fetishist about clean hair I've been washing it in buckets of cold drips from the ceiling, which doesn't do a lot for the morale. We've just had the Jehovah's Witnesses and someone's dropped a *Daily Telegraph* full of shit through the window of our cellar. I must have done something absolutely terrible in my last incarnation, as I heard the cashier at Sainsbury's say. Enough of this sordid tale – still, you did say you liked domestic details . . . I hope things have been better in London. What an over-long paragraph!

About Alan Ross – I don't think I'd better try any more on him. The last time I did, he sent me a Virago card as a rejection slip. Presumably he was not amused, like Queen Victoria. Personally, I love every form of wit from a custard-pie up or down (and usually down), but not everybody feels the same way.

I'm not quite sure when I'll be in London – February, I suppose. With my erratic lifestyle I find it hard to plan far ahead. Perhaps it would be best if I ring you a day or so before – it would be lovely if you're free for a chat again.

I'd better get on with some writing now in the only almost warm spot – reclining on the sofa by the fire. I always think better lying down, I don't know why. It must say something about my character!

                                 Yours,
                                 Fiona

At a previous meeting Hugo had told me that a long poem of his ('An Actor's War') and his parents' photograph would be appearing in the next edition of the *London Review of Books*.

26.4.85

Dear Hugo,

I tried to ring you this afternoon to say how much I liked your poem but, with my usual bad timing, I picked a moment when you were out.

I've only just got hold of my copy of the *LRB*; thanks to the wretched postal strike. Very frustrating! I was longing to see it, too, after you'd mentioned your parents would be on the cover and your poem inside. I kept rushing for the post first thing, hair on end and no make-up, etc. We don't have a letter-box in our abnormal house, so I have to open the door for anything too big to be slipped under. Eventually I rang the *LRB* and the bloke in the subscription dept. let out an awful snigger when he heard who I was. Still, I suppose a bad name's better than none! Anyway, your poem was well worth waiting for. If the rest are half as good, your book should be a big success. Your father comes across as such a wise, witty, likeable man – you've really made him live for me. How good-looking and happy your parents are on the cover too.

Things are pretty boring here. I'll have to take a trip soon to get away. My only entertainment's been the colourful stories in the local paper about difficult geriatrics being tied to commodes with crepe bandages in a councillor's rest home (I shouldn't laugh, but I can't help it); the leper who stabbed his flatmate with a Stanley knife (my mother scratched for days after reading that one as she has a leprosy phobia induced by reading Blackie's *Life of Christ* at the age of six); and, last but not least, how a local witch hexed Bexhill Light Opera's production of *Chu Chin Chow*. Life goes on.

Yours,
Fiona

I had taken to calling Hugo my 'Muse in the Angel' because
he lives in that area of Islington. The word 'former' was
added in the first line of this next letter because, even at this
stage, a feeling of strain had already entered the friendship.
The other people referred to in the letter are Jessica Gwynne,
the illustrator of Hugo's collection of poems *Love Life*, and
Andrew Motion, my editor at Chatto. The letter was written
at Christmas and accompanied by a water-colour of a white
kitten I'd painted for Hugo. She was dressed in suspender
belt, etc. and standing under the mistletoe in a feline brothel
with several tom-cat clients in various stages of undress. I was
particularly proud of the mistletoe. The feline card harked
back to a romantic phone call Hugo had once made,
comparing me to a sex-mad fluffy white kitten owned by his
mother in Portugal. (I regret giving this and two other hand-
painted Christmas cards to Hugo and have sometimes toyed
with the idea of asking for them back. At least I was able to
keep copies of the letters, so that I could put them to better
use.) Hugo's great-grandfather, mentioned halfway through
the letter, was a doctor in mid-Wales. He was called in to
treat a young girl who had been pretending that she could
survive on thin air. He had her watched and monitored,
stopping her thus from hiding scraps and berries for secret
eating. As a result the girl starved to death. The doctor
blamed himself so much that he hit on the bizarre notion of
giving up sex with his wife to punish himself. My poem
'Dildoes', mentioned towards the end of the letter, starts,
'Dildoes – they come in varied size and shape – /five foot, five
six, six foot, fair, middling, dark.' It goes on to compare
brainless men to dildoes and complains that I've never had a
real man, i.e., a thinking one. Unfortunately, a few thick male
readers tend to miss the joke and assume I'm still a virgin,
albeit one that plays around with six-foot-long dildoes.

Christmas '85

Dear Hugo,

This is just to wish my former Muse in the Angel a happy Christmas.

I keep rereading and enjoying bits of your *Writing Home*. I reckon you're one of the only poets who stands up to that – a lot of the stuff around now is so specious, derivative, meretricious, etc. that it goes phut on a second reading even if it looks impressive on the first. I suppose it's the quality of language used. I think your poem 'Going Round Afterwards' is one of my top favourites now. It's a pity your *Love Life*'s rather dismissed on the back cover – there are a lot of good poems there too, which hold up well in spite of the Jessica Gwynnes. Actually, I've mentioned *Love Life* briefly in one of the poems in my coming collection. Hope you don't mind a free advert?

My book seems to be progressing on schedule. The lolly on the cover's very indecent. I had a letter from Andrew saying, 'What's it remind you of . . . ?' I expect he regrets writing that now! He's got more daring now he uses the dictaphone. I'm really going to get accused of a phallic obsession as my previous collection was titled *The Tower of Glass*. (This wasn't my fault – the publisher wouldn't allow it to be called *A Cure For Impotence* after one of the other poems. I expect he was afraid a lot of impotent men would write in saying it hadn't cured them and threatening to sue him under the Trade Descriptions Act.) I've been accused of phallic obsessions before – at Chelsea School of Art. Once, when I put Nelson's Column in a picture! The other time, I asked for it more. We had to sling together a life-size figure in plaster in a week. (Very hard work!) The whole thing looked very abstract. I gave it a slightly long one in the hope that the statue might come alive in gratitude. The Cockney sculpture technician kept grabbing it and saying, 'Well, at least I've got a nice little handle to carry this chap by. . . .' Also, a couple of the blokes in my year started singing, 'Great balls of fire . . .' every time I came into a room for the rest of the term, or saying, 'Do you like cucumbers?' I eventually got them off that by telling them I only liked them thinly sliced and put in sandwiches – which wiped the smile off their faces.

I've still got the 'Sky Ray Lolly' poem in the book. I feel that perhaps you don't like it for psychological reasons – the bit about my having no urge to cook or clean and lacking maternal instincts. If it's any comfort, I do as much cooking and cleaning as most, I suppose. (I don't have to be perverted enough to like it, do I? Do you?) Also, I can be incredibly maternal to full-grown men, even if nappy-clad babies don't turn me on. I'd never slap or be sarcastic to kids, either – the things that most maternal types seem to do. I don't feel bound to do, or only do, womanly things, because I feel just as much a woman when I'm carrying a 70lb bag of plaster up the stairs, having a good swear at somebody or on the roof fixing slates. (I could never write as a man.)

I think I feel a similar psychological unease when I read your 'Sonny Jim' poems. (I hope you'll pardon this. It's probably almost as risky criticising someone's poetry as it is their sexual performance – something I wouldn't do.) I suppose I see Sonny Jim as your Mr Hyde side. The side that doesn't appreciate me and has treated me like a pest/fan/groupie that must be pushed to the most distant acquaintanceship. The side that's stopped saying 'Let me know when you're coming up to London and we'll meet', as you used to say. It's extremely hurtful to be pushed out of your life like this. I suppose your Sonny Jim side's like your medical great-grandfather – assuaging his own kinky sense of guilt by starving others emotionally.

Look, I'm not in the habit of reproaching men – there are plenty more bad fish near the sea. It's only because I'm fond of you, because I like you a lot, that I'm risking saying all this in the hope that it'll straighten things out. There's so much that's kind and nice and sensitive about you that I want you to be better than the rest. I feel the same about your writing. You must tell the truth and face up to things as they are to become a great rather than just a very good writer. You've got the wit, intelligence and technical ability – don't throw away what you have.

Maybe I've just used poor Sonny Jim in order to be able to say these things. I loved meeting and talking to you. I think I probably wrote better poems after. Still, seeing me obviously didn't mean much to you. Or am I misunderstanding things?

This letter's getting too serious for either my comfort or yours. To change the subject – I am now thirty-one. I think I should alter 'Dildoes' before submitting it with the newest poems to Andrew. 'I'm thirty-one, I've had no *real* man. . . .' The trouble with thinking men is they only seem able to think about it. Oh well, I'll have to console myself with a robot or two for Christmas. Poets may have better brains, but I reckon they're all ballsless. Am I right? (Don't worry, I'm only joking!) The funniest robotspiel I've heard recently came from a Persian I met on the train back from your reading. He/it wanted me to go back to his takeaway to see his miniature of Omar Khayyám painted on leather. A flask of HP, a burger and Thou. . . . I'm bored with junk food and junk men.

Hastings is as entertaining as ever. I saw another goat show – they were all in a smelly tent as it was raining. I renewed acquaintance with the one that kissed me last year. One of the Sussex Goat Club got in her pen and embraced her, saying, 'You're getting more like your auntie every day, my dear.' Other local events included readings by Raine and Patric Dickinson. A couple got turned on in C.R.'s 'Gauguin' and left. Given the lack of custom at the local family-planning clinic, there'll probably be consequences – hope they call it Craig Raine. Dickinson read himself to sleep – the best bit. His wife had to clap her hands to wake him. Lucky she was there supporting! Maybe you should include such an incident in your poem on growing old? Don't get too bitter, anyway. I'd be sorry to see that.

Re. growing old – people don't alter very much. The senile start senile, etc. I'd see you staying young and energetic. One of my art-school friends is senile at thirty-three. She plays bingo and also forced me to Bexhill, shopping. She'll be the life and soul of an old folks' home one day. She had seven stops to pee after a tea and coffee. I went twice, more out of boredom and

fellowship than necessity. She then had the cheek to say because I hadn't peed so often I *must* be unhealthy! People in-
variably accuse me of their own faults. I now judge others by
what they say of me – a good test. Next time you hear some
theory about my character, remember to apply it not to me, but
to the person who comes out with it.

I don't know if you remember my saying I was like my
great-aunt, who had stigmata? (It must be my paleness – she
died of a decline in her twenties.) Well, I'm also supposed to
look like my great-gran Lydia. She was in the habit of lying
around naked at eighty, liked young men, stout and jellied eels.
Perhaps I should follow her diet. I reckon, though, the secret of
staying young is having the humility to change. I'm determined
to grow old disgracefully and celebrate my sixty-ninth with a
69, etc.

You asked me when I was moving back to London. At the
moment, I don't make an income, let alone a *decent* income.
Prejudice being what it is, I never had a Gregory award – only
eighteen out of 134 went to women. I can get poems taken, but I
can't get a reading at all. I was turned down even for part of one
at the Poetry Society. X* had previously offered one, as well as
making an absolute pest of himself to me. When I tried to fix a
date for that reading, mentioning his promise, I was turned
down with a couple of really insulting letters from that bastard
Y.* He strikes me as the sort of person who only bothers to be
polite to the well-known. Anyway, without readings or awards,
I can't possibly make enough to live in London. I don't know
how many more years it'll take.

I still come up to London fortnightly (or more). I'm definitely
not on the invitation list for literary things, though, so coincidence (unaided by you, you heartless tease) may never bring us
together again – or not for years, anyway. By then, you'll be
older and wiser and I'll be older and wickeder. After looking at

---

* I have deleted the names of two officials of the Poetry Society in this
paragraph for obvious reasons.

the photo you took, I can see why you're afraid to meet me on my own these days. Do my eyes really turn red and flash fire when I look at you? Dear, dear, I didn't know I was that obvious.

I'll send you a copy of *Sky Ray Lolly* when it comes out. You won't have seen a lot of the poems as Andrew included most of the newest ones. I'm still very grateful for your advice on taking it back to Chatto, etc. I reckon it really helped.

You said once that we'd be friends for ages and ages. On the other hand, since spring you've behaved as if you want to get rid of me as all but the most distant acquaintance – the cancelled meetings, only writing/phoning because I'd sent work to the *New Statesman*. I don't believe you'd even have passed the time of day at the *London Review of Books* party if I hadn't spoken to you first. (You left it long enough.) Are my feelings of *no* account? Am I worth *nothing*? I honestly don't know what you want now. If you want to drop me, I wish I knew why, at any rate. Alternatively, if you *do* want my friendship (in this incarnation, not ages and ages hence), that's something you're going to have to fight for now. I'm tired of fighting. I'm too proud to do anything more unasked. I'm not going to drop you, though. You'll have to take the action, one way or the other. It's up to you.

Love,
Fiona

Hugo responded by asking me round. He seemed very depressed, so I sent him a packet containing various books, including my early collections, *London* (privately printed), *Rome* (Mammon Press) and *The Tower of Glass* (Mariscat Press) some funny cuttings and this next letter, hoping to cheer him up. The 'sunshine and 8s and 9s' mentioned signify luck and refer to a card Hugo sent me, which also contained a picture

of his father. Hugo's father, the actor Hugh Williams, was a
keen gambler and one of the card games he liked involved
lucky 8s and 9s. Hugo's reason for writing his 'Sonny Jim'
poems (mentioned at the end of the letter) was, he told me,
annoyance with his wife Hermine.

12.1.86

Dear Hugo,

Now you've got over your depressing Saturday, here's a sort
of literary tuck-box to cheer you up – I hope!

I was going to send you spare copies of my old booklets/
books when the newer, better collection comes out – trying
desperately to hide my inadequacies as ever. Anyway, you may
as well have them now – the books, I mean. *Some* of the poems
are OK, but less funny than the recent ones. Perhaps the *London*
ones are best – I don't know.

Thanks for your hospitality. You must come down for the day
and see the House of Usher (or rather, Pitt-Kethley) when it's
warmer and the regular winter gale-force 9 abates. It's a bit
sub-zero and leaky at the moment – nice weather for Eskimos.
I'm hardened to barefoot ordeals under drips on the marble, but
it would probably give anyone else instant influenza, bron-
chitis, pleurisy, etc.

Thanks also for the card. A nice thought – sunshine and 8s
and 9s. I'm very unlucky at cards.

I've got to do a twenty-minute after-lunch speech on the 8th
of May, before the Paternoster Club (I'm enclosing a leaflet
about the club). I'm allowed a guest – do you fancy coming with
me? The members are mostly ancient publishers, journalists,
etc., so maybe there'd be some useful contacts. I don't know yet
what I'll talk about; myself, probably – I'm like that. I'd better
write most of it down in case my memory fails after the food or I
get paralysed with fright.

I hope things go better at the *New Statesman*. My advice is to
pay no attention to *any* of the knockers. I think they're wrong
about your voice, also, which is a very good one by my standards. I've listened to plenty of preachers when I was young

and religious, and plenty of actors later. (I used to toy with the idea of going in for acting, standing at the backs of theatres for cheapness, seeing the same plays many times as an usher, etc. Eventually I realised that saying other people's words – often poor ones – would be a lot less creative and therefore less satisfying than writing my own.) Humans are a cruel lot and often criticise without real justification. I had a pretty rough time at school – one teacher told my mother I was deaf (she was and couldn't hear my replies); the Head insisted I was insane (she probably was as she regularly went to bed at seven and also boasted of remembering the place and name of each of the 700 of us at carol services for the last twenty years – could there have been space for anything else in her brain, I ask myself?); the school doc said I looked very unhealthy, then died a month after. I think if you stand out or are different from the herd, the beasts around you feel bound to locate some defect to explain it. They'd hate it to be that you're clever, talented, good-looking. Where would that leave them?

I'd love to see the poems you offered to send: 'The Pill', etc., 'Sonny Jim' even – now that I know your interesting reason for writing the SJs.

With love,
Fiona

David Medalla, the artist, mentioned at the end of my next letter, was the tutor in my poem 'A Piece of Jade' who brought into class some of his jade collection, including a piece designed for shoving up a corpse's arsehole to keep the evil spirits out. Hugo compared this artefact to the 'tamps' used by bears during their winter hibernation. As for Hugo's 'hair poems', he had written several poems on the subject, theorising that his hair might be a metaphor for his poetry and that the poems might one day be directly about poems.

Dear Hugo,

Glad you can manage May the 8th. What a lovely long letter to start my week off! I couldn't make up my mind whether to ring or write and say thank you for that and all the kind things you said about my work. Writing won. I never feel at my best on the phone – I can't modify what I'm saying with a smile or anything. I lack your brother's touch with hmms and huhs, etc.

Anyway, I shall ramble on (as usual!). No need to reply if you haven't got the time. I mustn't be selfish and waste your writing hours when you're hard-pressed during the term. Roll on the hols!

The ruddy *Tatler* now wants to snap me against Soho! With my luck it'll be pouring/snowing when they do it. Shame I don't own any black leather other than bags or shoes. I had an evil front-fastening suede mini, but it went missing years ago. My mother must have tidied it, or else it walked off. I can't find anything in this house. It's like a nightmare.

Chatto had said *The Tatler* wanted to come to Sussex, so I went round madly plastering holes in the hall, hiding rubbish in the no-go areas, etc. I even thought about going up a ladder to wash the Cupids near the front door. (We have several little plump darlings – in plaster, or something – sitting with garlands, about eight feet up above doors and panels in the hall. They are either cherubs or Cupids who've had their bows and arrows nicked. I prefer to think they're Cupids, and that washing them might be a kind of rite to Venus and son, for which I'll get suitably rewarded – i.e., preferably in this life and soon.) Then the woman from *The Tatler* rang. She sounded a bit dull and asked what my poems were about. Once she heard the word 'sex' she became determined to do me in my bedroom. I tried to explain that my bedroom wasn't that sort, so she asked where was the sex located then? I said much of the writing was generalisations. I also told her I grew up in London. Now the bloody woman thinks I'm a graduate of Soho. Anyway, I'd rather be thought a paid fallen woman than show her my bedroom, which has good old working-class black mould under the window, a naive-looking patchwork quilt, a bent curtain rail, cats' hair everywhere and ribbons of wallpaper hanging like jungle creepers from the ceiling since I replastered the four-foot-by-two hole which suddenly appeared there. (The things I do! My biceps have to be felt to be believed.) Now, if I'd had black satin sheets, a tiger skin and a four-poster, they could have snapped me in bed with my blessing.

Talking about romantic bedrooms, I recently came across a seaside landlady who runs a sort of honeymoon hotel. She advertises 'Victorian Cream Teas', continental breakfasts, Nottingham lace four-posters and several varieties of hen roaming the back garden to keep the kiddies occupied.

To answer your questions about the books – yes, I did draw (copy) the bit on Rome from some seal of Augustus pictured in a history book. I'm hoping nobody'll realise, though, as I'm sorry I had any part in the vile design of the book. I'm not a graphic artist by temperament; I trained in painting. Mammon Press covers are usually *even worse*, which was what tempted me to have a bash. Luckily you know I can do better with suggestive Christmas cards of cats. The Mariscat cat *is* the publisher's symbol – he lives in Mariscat Road. The nicer cover on this book is a woodcut from some old bibliography which he found. I expect the picture *is* all about downfall after sex – not that I agree with that philosophy. I've never been able to whip up any guilty feelings about sex – one reason I'm not religious these days. It seems too pleasant to be wrong. I can't think why people get punished for it in novels.

I'm a bit worried about being compared to a bacon-slicer in your letter. Really, Hugo I'm not the castrating type of woman – I haven't even had my tom cat done! (He modelled for the one with the eye-glass and money on your Xmas card.) My father had an awful joke about a man who fancied a bacon-slicer, but I'd better not tell you it. Seriously though, if I like a poet's work generally, there's no way I'm going to hate, or be vilely critical about, a part of it. As I said to someone the other day, sex is never bad, only good, better, best. I'm sure the same's true of your poems. (No, you're definitely not a plagiarist, you've an original and very subtle voice. Anybody who can read assimilates elements of other people's work – it's dishing them out in your own way that counts. I'm sure fashion *is* important not trivial. I'm probably totally concerned with it too, in the sense of trying to find the spirit of the times, to see what's coming, etc. I think your poems have the quality mentioned in 'Dégagé' – the good taste coming through later. This'll probably win you more admirers in the long run, but less comps in the short. Did your father have a different theory of dress for women, I wonder? Are we allowed to knock 'em dead in red in seconds? Or is that vulgar? It probably is. I've done more than my fair share of vulgar things, come to think of it. I'm getting better, though. Maybe I'll be refined by the time I'm a hundred. As your hair poems will be about poems one day, so will my sex ones – but not yet!)

Talking about sex – funny, I can't keep off the subject – I loved your misconceptions about it in your nice prep-school article, which I came across a few months back. I knew all about it young, due to all the telling finger gestures going round my school and the company I kept at the local park. When I was a toddler, though, I thought people excreted babies. I'd probably heard someone calling their kid a little shit. I also thought tampons might be kits for making toy mice. You cover one with fur or felt and let the tail hang out (well, I was nearly right), then give it to the church bazaar.

From tampons to tamps – thanks for the natural history lesson. I reckon the bears should raid David Medalla's museum and winter in style with jade suppositories. I'm sorry this letter's getting lower and lower. I'll have to go and take a cold shower under some leaky ceiling.

                        With love,
                        Fiona

The following letter was sent with a copy of *Sky Ray Lolly*, I had just been to Hugo's house for tea and he had given me copies of his early books, which I didn't have. He also lent me his family tree (in fact he tried to give it to me), as I had an inkling that we might be related. Hugo's great-grandfather, Hugh Williams, was a colourful character in Welsh social history. He wrote and collected Chartist songs and, in his capacity as a lawyer, defended a great many of the rioters successfully. Some people even identified him with the anonymous 'Rebecca', the inciter of the Rebecca Riots. My comment about 'Uncle Sam' being less moral is a joke, referring to the fact that Hugh was also known as 'Hugh of the Hundred Bastards'. On the negative side, he was grabbing when it came to property. There's a dubious-sounding case recorded of a lessee on his land having to move on. Hugh's first marriage was to a woman twenty-five years older – obviously for money. Hugo claimed that he did not consummate that marriage. His wife, to punish him, lived to be ninety or so. His second wife, in his own old age, was by contrast a young girl. It is from this marriage that Hugo is descended.

21.3.86

Dear Hugo,

Here's your personalised copy.

Thanks for the books. I'm really pleased to have them. I can study you properly now, not just be tantalised by remembering bits inaccurately. That's a nice photo inside the *Symptoms of Loss* cover – still very like. I'll put it with my pin-ups, I think.

I've enjoyed having a snoop through your family tree; it beats looking at a man's etchings any day. Once I saw the outside of the envelope I realised that I had read about your Chartist great-grandfather years ago when I was looking up some Welsh history. I've copied a bit on him – it's from Hastings Library's copy of the *Dictionary of Welsh Biography*. I know I've read other

things about him too – probably in some history of Carmarthen.
If I ever come across them again I'll copy them for you.

My great-great-great-uncle David Evans helped burn toll
gates in the Rebecca Riots mentioned in the piece. He never got
caught as his family hid him. My mother thinks that he *might*
have been the grandson of the David Evans at the top of your
tree. She's not sure, though, as she only picked up snippets of
info when a small child, from the family black sheep, her
great-uncle Samuel Williams. Her 'Uncle Sam' was decidedly
less moral than your Chartist ancestor, by the way. I have
inherited the exact shape of his thumbs, which is supposed to
be a bad sign.

I'm looking forward to *This Is Your Life*.* Hope you enjoy the
enclosed *Sky Ray Lolly* – preferably to be read in bed by the light
of a torch.

With love from Fiona

In the following letter, Bernard Stone is the owner of the
Turret Bookshop and also the publisher of Turret Books. The
Caledonian Hotel was the venue for a literary lunch where I
gave a speech; Hugo had come as my guest. Neil Rennie is an
old friend of Hugo's.

15.5.86

Dear Hugo,

I've just done my deal with Bernard Stone – no 'horny
hands', you'll be glad to hear, and not that many nude pics in
his office.

Sorry I missed you today – I should have booked ahead!

---

* Hugo's actor brother Simon was about to be surprised on the TV pro-
gramme *This Is Your Life*.

I keep seeing tartan spots before my eyes since the Caledonian. My father would have liked that place. Oh dear, I was so hoping to take you to a swish do. All my plots about you seem to go awry. One of these days I'll get things right. I *was* glad to have you there, though – it's much more fun having someone to talk these odd things over with after. The man on my right at lunch told me he'd never manage to remember my name and then said no more!

Thanks for all the support you've given me there and at the other readings. I really appreciate that. I'm often more insecure and frightened underneath than I seem. It's wonderful to feel there's someone really on my side.

Here are the copies I promised. Maybe I'll find some more next time I look through a few history books. While scouring the Williamses in various tomes I even found strange stuff on my own hymn-writing ancestor.* It seems he set up marriage-guidance groups in the eighteenth century!

I really enjoyed our saunter round Soho/Chinatown in the rain. Maybe I ought to learn how to make bean cakes. Those Chinese–English recipes are so peculiar, though. I once bought a packet of vermicelli for 50p from the Loon Moon, which said under 'Cooking Instructions' that you could give it as presents to amaze your friends. (Well, I'd be amazed if someone gave me a handful, wouldn't you?)

I like your idea of going with Neil Rennie to the last live show in Soho before the great close-down. Shall I come too and hold your hand/hands in the back row?

I expect I'll be in London in a week or two – before the end of May, anyway. If you're free and want to meet up before you disappear to Ireland, Switzerland, Brittany and Portugal (or before I disappear for months if I do that travel book), give me a ring. Or, I might give you one – I'm getting very predatory in my old age. That reminds me – what was that about your hoping youth and 'crabbed age' could live together? I expect

---

* William Williams of Pantycelyn.

you mean to take up with some sixteen-year-old once you get
your old-age pension, and go on dirty weekends arranged by
Saga. What a shame – I was counting on coming round to you
in my wheelchair when we're both old and senile. I'm sad to
find you're planning to cast me off for a much younger woman.
What must I do to please you – take monkey glands or dress up
in a school uniform? Well, maybe I could try the uniform. . . . Is
there any hope for me?

With love from Fiona

Hugo's daughter Murphy had just returned to university after
a family row. 'Mandi', referred to at the beginning of this
letter, had sent some rather poor poems to the *New Statesman*,
together with a cutting about herself from a local newspaper,
all of which Hugo passed on to me for a joke.

Undated letter (possibly late May or early June 1986)
Dear Hugo,
I've just got your letter – it had been held up over the Bank
Holiday weekend. Mandi, of course, is simply your average
Sussex clone; there are a lot of them in Hastings – they're just
older, fatter and madder here.
Here's my local interview – I only got one pic, not two like
Mandi. I look really stuck up. Still, the stairs look all right. I fear
I've been misquoted – where's this rush of readings? I'll be in
real trouble if any feminists get hold of this, won't I? Well, I
don't mind girls on Page 3, I'd just like some naked men on page
2 to keep them company.
I've been thinking over the things you were saying. I'm a bit
too slow to react sometimes. Can a screwed-up woman like me
– please forgive me if I'm saying too much – give some advice?
Why not make the first move and get in touch with Murphy,
even if you wrote or rang last? I've just remembered that I used

to sleep late simply because I felt that life wasn't worth getting up for I was so damn depressed. Don't let her feel cut off now – be there for her. I hate to see people who are really fond of each other drifting apart.

While I'm being personal and interfering, I don't believe you're a cold fish any more than I am. We're both capable enough of love. You've been hurt a lot, it seems to me. I know *I'm* terrified of showing love in case it's thrown back at me. I keep joking about it to give myself a face-saving way out.

I don't believe, either, that you can have been a boring husband; good-looking, clever, kind, witty – what more does she want? I've never found you boring – not for one minute. Why do you think I keep ringing, writing, making you cakes, harassing you, etc? Most men I'm happy to lose quickly. Most of them *really are* boring. You're the only one to get the star treatment!

I'd better stop this very personal letter right away. I'm in London next Thursday for a lunchtime launch of that Feminist Book Fortnight. I hope I don't get harassed by any lesbians. (Somebody sent me intense poems about her clitoris the other day. . . . I wonder. . . .) But you've got your workshop then, so I don't suppose I'll see you till you come to St Leonards in August.

I hope you enjoy Ireland. (When I was in Cork I saw a stuffed cow in a shop in the docks – just the cow, nothing else, no sign, no price, no explanation!) I hope you have a good rest with your mum in Portugal and write lots of wonderful poems. The one based on the letters about Belsen, etc. sounds a great idea. I'll really miss you.

With all the love I'm capable of!
Fiona

PS Mind Hermine's glass-crunching flasher friend doesn't paint your house pink while you're away.*

---

* Hermine was staying home while Hugo was in Portugal. A theatrical friend of hers, who was in the habit of performing a rather strange avant-garde act, had been hired to mend the roof and paint the window-frames while Hugo was away.

In the next letter an accident suffered by Hugo is referred to.
He broke a bone in his foot and would not go to a doctor to
have it set. He was convinced he could set it himself by
putting the foot into the right position. He claimed that
wearing a pair of 'brothel-creepers' in plum and black suede,
a size too large, was responsible. The French mistranslation
referred to is one sent me after a listener on the other side of
the Channel had heard me reading 'The Fear of Splitting Up'
on Radio 4. (He misheard 'lotus position' as 'locust position'.)

                                    Undated letter (June 1986)
Dear Hugo,
   I'm happy to hear things are better now with Murphy. I
expect she's very fond of you, coming over like that.
   I was so sorry to hear about your foot, though. The feet or
hands seem extra susceptible to pain. It's awful that happening
just before you had to go away. I should rest as much as you
can; don't walk on it too much, and eat well to keep your
strength up. Oh, I sound like a nurse, don't I? I do worry about
you, though. Get better soon and come back fighting fit.
   Here's the mad Frenchman's mistranslation. I'm thinking
about trying the locust position if I can find any takers. For
another laugh, here's that *Standard* piece. Valerie Grove has
copied the *Observer* mistake and made my mum thirty-nine
when she married. People have been asking me about that. I
say, 'I may be a bastard, but I'm not illegitimate.' I expect this
letter'll lie around for weeks waiting for you to come back now.

                                    Love,
                                    Fiona

The next letter worth including was written after a quarrel. The seagull referred to is one I named after Hugo. Seagulls tend to find cheese aphrodisiac.

Undated (late September 1986, after my first research trip to Italy for the book *Journeys to the Underworld*)

Dear Hugo,

Glad we're friends again. Are any of these possibilities for the *New Statesman*? Nothing about you this time. Maybe I ought to write one about that seagull – I'm still calling him to my bedroom window for food. Hugo (that Hugo) performs wonders on a lump of cheese.

So you say you only have it off with brainless women?* Shame on you! I've been looking for a beautiful brainy man all my life. Can I *pretend* to be brainless perhaps? I'm a good actress. Does my writing about sex all the time qualify me as brainless?

Italy, as ever, proved a fertile soil for brainless men. I think I shall devote a chapter to Neapolitan erections. I had a wonderfully inane conversation in bad Italian about the size of some idiot's cock, which I may quote in full in the book. Archaeological perverts rate another chapter. Do you know, I actually met a man who wanted me to sink my teeth into his cock in the Baths of Venus at Baia? I should have thought the idea of that would make most men run screaming home to Mum. He had to settle for a go with my mother-of-pearl necklace – the next best thing. Another chapter, I think, for the Sicilian who offered me the whole of his heart, half his *pensione* and motor-boat business, and a three-month tour of various countries. The snag was I'd have had to be his wife and live on a volcano with only a

---

* Hugo had once said this as a joke.

piano bar and baseball club for entertainment. Perhaps I should also do a chapter on the world's worst lover (French). That shattered my illusions – I thought they were supposed to be good at it. I once had a gym teacher who shattered my illusions about athletic stamina.

Talking about fantasies, Bernard Stone fancies having it off with a contortionist. I told him she'd probably be a great disappointment (like the gym teacher), as most positions feel much the same. Do you fancy contortionists? ('The lotus is no problem' and I can even just about get my feet behind my head. I have this brainless *alter ego* called Sunny Jemima who likes doing things like that.)

Now *I* have a foolish fantasy about having an intelligent man. (The only kink I haven't tried.) I keep thinking he might be more sensitive and less of an unkind graceless clod than the rest. But maybe I'm wrong. Will we ever come together in some pause between your search for sex dolls and my pursuit of dildoes?

Unlike you I'd love to mix friendship and sex. I've only had jerks, bores and bastards so far. Thank God I didn't get any of them pregnant. Can sex kill friendship? I can't imagine it would – not if vitriolic poems don't. Maybe if people can talk to each other they've got more chance of getting things right in the end.

With love and lust,
Fiona

19.12.86

Dear Hugo,
    You say I have many talents – ah, but you haven't tried my singing, my chocolate gingerbread cake or my. . . . You ain't seen nothing yet.
    Thanks for your letter. Have a good time at your brother's.
    No, I haven't been asked to the *TLS* bash. They don't like me

and nobody asks me to lit. parties these days – haven't been asked to one since May or June. Do you think they can be ostracising me because I'm a wanton woman? (Well, wanton-ish. . . .) Do you detect my Christmas misanthropy (and mis-ogyny) setting in? Bugger Father Christmas, bugger stockings, bugger tinsel, bugger everything. I think I'll go and stuff a turkey, as the sex maniac said. I *ought* to go on the roof and do some repairs. God's taking a leak through all our balconies again – hardly enough buckets and frying-pans to go round. Life is fun in St Leonards.

Last week I did my good deed for the year and rescued a blackbird that I found sighing under a car. I put it in a box and walked miles to the Sheba Bird Sanctuary – got lost and had to get a nun in civvies in a Catholic school up a hill to ring the owner for me to find where it was. Eventually I found the place: a tiny railway cottage, cat on a cushion just inside the door, two black greyhounds behind, eleven more cats and two built-in aviaries full of parakeets in the front room. The bird will re-cover, I'm told, after they've syringed its neck. Birds' necks swell when they're knocked down by a car or something, mak-ing their heads hang down with their beaks almost touching the ground – most pathetic. It's too much like hard work rescuing things (and catching them), though. I think I might pass by on the other side next time.

What else has happened in my wildly exciting life? A fan offered me a week in Barcelona – he said his three-wheeled car would tip over if he went alone.

Don't wish me peace and quiet for Christmas – I want lust and money (preferably untaxable). Lust I never seem to get in the festive season; spring, summer, autumn, maybe – Christmas, never. I suppose the British are all too cold to take their pants off at Yuletide. I once put a note in Santa's box in a shop asking for a good fuck for Xmas. I spelt it wrong and wrote it in green crayon to look as if some kid had done it.

Listen, my Muse, my poetry is flagging. I haven't written a whole poem for weeks. I can manage good lines but have no ability to structure at the moment. I'm trying to do one on

AIDS, one on Mills and Boon. Perhaps the subjects lack cha-
risma? I hope I'm not on the scrap-heap at thirty-two – going on
holiday and prose-writing must have turned me brainless. Inspire me, please, when you get back!

With love,
Fiona

Hugo and I next met in January, I was very depressed as
several ceilings had fallen in and I'd spent a great deal of time
carrying out buckets of soggy plaster to bury in the snowy
garden. Part of one ceiling fell on my typewriter and various
beginnings of poems written in ink became so sodden that
they were unreadable. Hoping to cheer myself up, I decided
to risk making a verbal pass at Hugo. He told me he despised
me thoroughly and then dropped me. In the autumn of 1987,
after meeting me by chance at the Poetry Society, he wrote
apologising for the things he'd said and our friendship was
resumed. This is the letter I wrote in reply.

15.10.87

Dear Hugo,
   Yes, of course, let's wipe the slate clean. Maybe we'd better
make a pact to *try* not to hurt each other any more. One day –
six months or ten years on – I'll risk showing you affection
again, when I'm sure you won't despise me for it. I'm just a
good-time girl in search of fun, basically. I liked best the times
when the non-personal repartee flowed on both sides. I love to
talk to witty people and there aren't many of us around. Let's
agree only to attack others in future. (Who do you want me to
bitch about?)
   I won't offer to drop the poems I've written on you, as they're
good and I'm short of work, slowing down and only halfway
towards the next book. My best offer's that I can always pretend

they're about someone else! The *London Review of Books* one was the only one in which I spilled confidences – remember I was mad as hell when I did it and remember who maddened me. The *LRB* has just turned against me, if it's any comfort. They got me to do a verse reply to a poem of Clive James's, then wouldn't print it. They thought I was even more sexist than he was. I had the bad taste to demand payment from them anyway.

I have just had a Welsh tour: seven readings in four days – a positive assault course in humiliation. If you think Hastings is bad for poets, try Swansea. I had an audience of *one* – an unemployed playwright who wanted the full reading and his money's worth. To top it all, somebody was on the roof using a chainsaw at the time! Still, I got my cheque – the important bit. My last reading was in Carmarthen; I didn't have the address and the organiser failed to meet me at the station. It turned out that I had to read in a pub in Lammas Street and also stay in a hotel there. Either could have been the inn David Evans, your ancestor and, I think, mine, used to keep nigh on 200 years ago. There were only four pubs in the street and it *had* to be one of them! A very strange coincidence. Carmarthen market had a lovely egg stall run by a crone. She had photos of who'd laid what on all the boxes – bantams, Aylesbury ducks, etc.

Just before we wipe the slate – re. cancelling dates. . . . It's OK if it's for work or illness, but *not* OK when you've decided to go off with someone else. That's a way of saying you're more important, or your time's more important than mine. I'm sure your other friends *also* find this offensive. They're probably just too arse-lickerish to say so. Perhaps they don't like to cross a well-known writer or someone who's been to Eton. I'm not like that – I'd tell Prince Charles to fuck himself if he offended me. I've got too much self-respect to fear anyone.

Another point: although I hate the kind of feminism that worries about Cockney fruit-sellers calling women 'darling', I am fighting for the sort that means I can show affection freely without being despised. (I don't despise men who've shown they're fond of me – I'm fond of them back.) Women should be able to be good friends to men or each other. Anything else is *old-fashioned* and less than human. Let's all have a truce in the war of the sexes.

There's no need to reply to this long long letter. It's just to say your apologies are accepted and everything's all right again. I will be in touch and have that drink soon. I have been out too much lately, though, and desperately need to stick at home and get some writing done. In a week or two, I'll give you a ring and leave a very long pause so that you have to ask me out. If you fail to do so, expect the direst of revenges – all that I had planned before you wrote. Amongst other things, I could offer a prize of a Mars bar every time I perform 'Just Good Friends', for the first person in the audience who can guess the literary hero. Do you like Mars bars, by the way?

Love,
Fiona

PS 'Yours cravenly, but sincerely' is fine, but never repeat *never* end your letters 'Best wishes' – like the previous one.

Hugo's initial reply was probably the funniest he ever sent. It consisted of a Portuguese Catholic picture of an extremely pious boy kneeling and taking his first communion from the Saviour. The boy had a huge white bow on his arm. Hugo said that he would be like the boy in the picture and signed it: 'A well-known writer who's been to Eton'. In his next letter he wrote saying that he'd been asked to give a reading at Newport straight after a workshop at Stevenage and was wondering if he'd get there on time. I replied with inside information. He also sent a book on rune-casting that he thought I might like, as I'd read his tarot cards at our making-up drink. The mention of the one-armed men refers back to some peculiar poems someone had submitted to him at the *New Statesman* and which he had passed on to me for a laugh.

14.11.87

Dear Hugo,

On the wings of something or other – also I thought you'd need some advice. I have done Newport. Are you in the Arts Centre? It's very big and prestigious, includes swimming baths, etc., but they don't come for the poetry. (Not for mine, anyway.) The woman who runs the arts side is nice and told me the tale of how popular the saunas had become since a councillor stroked someone's thigh in there and the case got in the papers. I felt like suggesting my small audience adjourned to the sauna. I love saunas, do you? I like looking at (and feeling superior to) all the fleshy architectural monsters unleashed from their corsets, but I haven't yet felt moved to stroke their thighs.

The train service to Newport is good. Perhaps you'd better have a headache at Stevenage, get back to London quickly, cut across to Paddington and on to the InterCity for Swansea?

God, some organisers are mean! In September, in Southampton, I had a spectacular coughing fit in the midst of two poems and the buggers didn't even buy me a drink. Anyway, readings are all money to write more poetry. Many thanks for the books. An advance birthday present? I'll try to master it and incorporate it into my fortune-telling. There are some great quotes: 'As one long-time rune-caster put it, "If I'm in for heavy water, I can put on my long underwear when I get up."'

I like the thought of Rune Play:

(2) Stand in front of a mirror and make F by stretching.

(3) Do it while floating in a pool, hot tub or ample bathtub, a river, a lake, the ocean. . . .

(7) Let the last image you hold in your mind before you drift off to sleep be F.

(Yes, please.)

I am doing your horoscope! Slowly. I'm not very experienced and may need to take a little advice from an astrologer who sent me a rude poem the other day. I shall reveal all at Christmas.

Anyway, you will certainly be a lot more famous than now, in time. I really want that for you. (I'm not every Tom, Dick or Harry's fan!) I have a feeling there'll be much more notice taken of you with the *Selected* and your next book. (It's long overdue.)

I haven't yet seen the *London Magazine* bit, but I'm not too worried – I had a reasonable one in *Elle* the other day. Mags only like to do articles about me because I project a coherently peculiar persona. I've been hoping somebody'd make dirty jokes about my private parts in a review, but they're all too goddam polite.

I am going to the 'Mr Hastings' contest tonight. Should be funny!

Tomorrow, I go to the opening (with drinks) of a local woman's shop. She plans to sell antiques *plus* very expensive Basque corsets made to old designs. I don't think they'll do too well in St Leonards. Before that I must go up a ladder and put lead on my belfry. God, I'm sick of this house. I don't mind Andrew Motion winning the Dylan Thomas – could have been worse, could have been an enemy – but I would like a good dollop of money so I have enough for a sordid bedsit in lovely London. I think I'll try for an Arts Council grant.

Re. one-armed men – never fancied an amputee, but I'm quite happy with men who only use one at a time. Fun getting my arms round, or rather hands on, a 'well-known writer who's been to Eton' last week, even if it was only so that I didn't fall off his bike.

Right, now I must polish off the Italian book, put lead on the belfry if the bats haven't moved in, and finish your horoscope.

See you soon – in the flesh or in my dreams.

With love,
F.

                                                                    11.12.87

Dear Hugo,

Just a short one – life's hectic. I wish somebody'd give us all an amnesty on Christmas.

What's this about Indians and squalid sofas?* I haven't had a free meal after a reading since Feb. I don't have another reading till March now, and even that's not firm.

How do you like the prophet on the reverse? He wrote a four-liner about an AIDS-infected fart and recited it to some old ladies down here. I've got some peculiar poem cards about pee and bagpipes from him – I'll show you when I can find them.

I'm very glad you were off at Newport that particular Wednesday. Otherwise you might have been coming back via Kings Cross at the wrong moment. I kept thinking that while I watched the horrors on the News. Tubes will never feel the same again.

Love,
Fiona

PS Mum's comment on reading the travel MS: 'I don't mind the affairs, but why did you have to say our kitchen was stinking?'

My next letter accompanied Hugo's horoscope.

                                                                    18.12.87

Dear Hugo,

Here comes the awful truth about yourself as written in the stars. . . . Happy Christmas.

I like playing the who's-like-who-on-TV game too. Yes, John

---

* Hugo had said that he was usually given an Indian meal and made to sleep on someone's squalid sofa after a reading.

Lloyd is a Fred McMurray. I'd thought that in the past. Anouk Aimée and Hermine? The only resemblance is the nationality. Your wife reminds me in some ways of the late Joan Greenwood.

Now, here's a challenge – who am I like? (Remember, if you say anything unflattering I'll fucking flatten you.) Talking of resemblances, I had late-night encounters with clones of you and Hermine in Italy (separately). It's all gone in the book. I have also mentioned you by name there in another context. . . .

I've just finished the travel epic and feel totally exhausted, having relived it all as I wrote. I expect Andrew * will have a lurid Christmas with my packet in plain wrappers to stimulate him.

Love,
Fiona

Hugo's bike had been stolen, I wrote sympathising about that and also about various health problems he'd mentioned.

12.1.88

Dear Hugo,
I am really *really* sorry about your beautiful bike. Why can't thieves stick to taking them from showrooms or doing bank robberies? I hope you were well insured. Talking of insurance, we are still trying to get blood out of a stone (Sun Alliance) after the hurricane.

I'm a hypochondriac too. I think everybody ought to be one. We've all got built-in obsolescence. The only way to get the better of our own particular area of weakness is to be hypochondriac enough to catch the illnesses at the earliest stage. I reckon herbs and hypochondria go together like a Mills and a Boon. I

---

* Andrew Motion, Poetry Editor at Chatto & Windus.

get a lot of quiet enjoyment out of trying experimental cures on myself. Sometimes, when I read a medieval Welsh treatment for a sore throat or whatever, I'm really sorry to have to wait a year before I can use it. Herb teas work wonderfully well on the things doctors can't find proper cures for – conditions. The more I see of what doctors have done in the way of killing off, or of making people's lives a misery with their over-harsh treatments, the less I want to go near them. Some of them dish out steroids like bloody Smarties.

I can get asthma, migraines and rheumatism as a sort of allergy to foodstuffs. I can control these to almost nothing by taking the appropriate herbs and having a fairly simple diet. I spotted that E additives, salt, white sugar and white flour weren't good for you as a child, long before the bumbling medical profession got round to them. I don't find the odd lapse does much harm, as long as most of the regular diet's pure. (I don't want to be a crank and refuse everything when out to dinner.) I'm going on about my slight problems in case those you mention might be curable by this technique. It's such a misery when the body turns against its owner.

As one medically unqualified hypochondriac to another – cut down on alcohol and coffee, drink lots of Perrier or other mineral waters, barley water plus herb teas, if you can stand it. If you want something that stimulates the way coffee does, the nearest's peppermint – not as good, but a slight lift plus mild pain-killer and pleasant-tasting. Rosemary tastes odder, but stimulates the heart and circulation, so gives a boost. (It's also a remarkable cure for tonsilitis.) It's not easy to beat coffee, alas. Try your sage. Did you know a man cannot die with that in his garden? (Old proverb.) It's also good for chest and throat. I always take it before readings – it makes the voice as clear as a bell. The only trouble is I have to keep going for a pee first. The other one for cystitis is marshmallow – leaves or flowers. The flowers make an attractive cherry-coloured tea. Diuretic foods are chiefly asparagus, parsley, celery and fennel. I once had a dream in which your father appeared and told me to tell you to take fennel. I didn't like to pass on the message before in case you thought I was mad. (You probably do now, after all this long rigmarole.)

I can't vouch for prostate-improving herbs, obviously. One book at home recommends sarsaparilla. Apparently this contains the equivalent of the male hormone testosterone. (So that's what I was drinking as a kid.) My dad used to take me to a wonderful herbalist's (for the soft drinks): Baldwin's in the Elephant and Castle. I don't know if it still exists. It was all Victorian – mahogany shelves full of jars of leaves, liquorice, etc., tiles and brass herbal-beer pulls. You could get a pint of sarsaparilla drawn by a dour barmaid. They had softened water so the sarsaparilla had a good head on it. My father got a herbal-beer kit there and inflicted what he termed 'a drink' on some of my friends' parents. (He was teetotal.) I think they thought they were getting sherry. You should have seen their faces. Everybody at school thought I was very low after that. (Probably right.)

Talking about low, feel free to lower the tone and talk about your bladder any time we're together. I can talk about my . . . well, perhaps not. I am decent enough not to spill beans on such matters where friends are concerned. I like your sort of first-memory poem about peeing out freely – very cosmic. Is it going in your *Selected*?

Now, about myself – nice comparisons. Theda Bara must be right – I've heard that before. Nell Gwynne, I'm told, too. Sometimes resemblances last only for a haircut. I had six months of cloning Barbara Dickson – now, not at all. I've decided to stop being demure in '88 – Jane Austen may go. Stand by for the sexier Fiona. I've been too pure all my life.

I can't find a spot-on resemblance for you on TV. I think there's a bit of Rupert Everett/Tom Bell/Robert Powell – oh, and of course, Alain Delon, whom you mentioned in a poem. I expect A.D.'s shorter, though – those French are. Re. lookalikes – I can't remember Hank Williams/Lord Home. How about Geoffrey 'dead sheep' Howe and Peter Porter?

Yes, you've a bright friend in Neil Rennie. He's got a brighter friend in you, though. He can't write as well. Still, he's a nice man. He talked very admiringly of you at your party. I'd sense some psychic ability there – Scottish second sight, telepathy perhaps. I still reckon you're the cleverest person I've met. I feel tempted to 'use' you in the way you 'use' Neil Rennie because of this. I've always worshipped wisdom. Perhaps it's only women in whom you don't look for intelligence enough. Aren't I better than a ruddy travel agent who 'fixes tours for Middle-Eastern VIPs'? I'd at least have sold them Tower Bridge while I had them at my mercy.

You wish me as much 'love and success and peace to write' in '88 as I wish you. OK, in the spirit of our fortunes being parallel, *I* wish *you* a steadily increasing flow of money, jobs, fame, success (especially when the new book comes out), peace to write poems, more of the respect you're due from the literary world, better health and *love* – ah yes, here I wish you what I'd wish myself, lots of kisses, cuddles and sex with the one person in the world you'd choose above all others. I can't say more than that, can I?

Love,
Fiona

Hugo had been forced to leave his job as TV critic of the *New Statesman*. He was wondering about making ends meet and suggested that going mad might solve his problems.

27.1.88

Dear Hugo,

I really admired your speedboat poem. (Always knew you were fast.) You're definitely on top form with 'The Slide' and this. Obviously I'm right in what I say of your intelligence. Only the really clever go on developing. Other people deteriorate fast from their early twenties on. 'Self Portrait with a Speedboat' is wonderful – I keep rereading it. It works on all sorts of different metaphysical levels. With these, 'Sonny Jim in Carnaby Street' and 'Prayer', your next book of new poems should be the best yet. You're light years ahead of most of the poets around.

Winning the race, but crashing in 1980?* Did anything awful happen in '80? Perhaps I'm being too literal-minded. *I* still see you going onward and upward.

Like you I mostly have flawless health – so no need for sympathy. I've more or less cured the things I've mentioned. Herbs rule OK – besides, a girl's got to have a hobby. Re. 'unpredictable erection inhibitions' – worrying for *you*, yes, but let me assure you, no woman with the faintest trace of the 'milk of human kindness' would mind about that. I wouldn't mind. Don't let this spoil your lifestyle. I notice you have a touch of stage-fright before readings although you have a beautiful voice. Believe in yourself. Now, if you think I'm cranky about herbs and diet, how about a yoga breathing exercise? This is guaranteed to reduce stress before readings, bank managers, doctors and all other fear-inducing pisspots. Breathe up one nostril to a slow count of five, hold it for five, then out of the other for five, up that one again for five, etc. You get the idea? It's hobby-time for hypochondriacs. Seriously, you *should* believe in yourself more. I think you're lovely and I've got very good taste. (BA Hons in Fine Art = certificate to *prove* I know about beauty.)

Sorry to hear you're not 'drinkable' – nice word. When the *TLS* pieces are all safely gathered in, perhaps? I'm always drinkable where you're concerned. I always miss you a lot. My other friends aren't a patch on you, I've decided. Good ideas for the future – can I take you for a drink at the Lesbian Centre† on your birthday, or propose on the 29th? If you're not free then, I can always save those up for later. No need to answer this if

---

* These were metaphors in Hugo's 'Speedboat' poem.

† Hugo had written me two letters on headed 'Gay and Lesbian Centre' paper, while assuring me he wasn't gay. I joked that he must be a lesbian then, and hinted it could be 'the start of a beautiful relationship'.

you're busy – when you're ready. I promise to be understanding. . . . Don't go mad, though. You went mad last year when you dropped me. I couldn't bear any more of that.

Love,
Fiona

I wrote the next letter after Hugo had referred in his 'Freelance' column in the *Times Literary Supplement* to my reading the poem 'Prostitution', which runs down my publisher at that stage (Chatto and Windus), on Channel Four's *Comment*.

25.2.88

Dear Hugo,

Thanks for the *TLS* plug – a witty article. Chatto/Andrew, etc. have ignored *Comment*, so I'm glad your column will rub in the points. Prose lasts longer than TV. (Chatto still hasn't paid me!)

Thinking about Hermine's troubles, although it's bad about the small advance, I suppose the fact that she's not a professional writer alters the situation. When poets with years of skill and experience and a proven track record behind them are paid like cleaners (or worse), then that really is a scandal. Anyway, let me know when Hermine's book comes out and I'll ask the London Library to order it.

I've been trying to get a high-powered agent to represent me in my search for more cash. I met Douglas Adams on a radio chat show two or three months ago and we got on very well, so he recommended me to his. Unfortunately, Ed Victor's still dithering and can't make up his mind.

I have been pondering what you said about a possible reason for my not getting readings, adjudications, awards and British Council jaunts. (Oh, I'd love to be going to Israel with you. Sod cruel Fate!) You think I'm not 'affable'? (Watch it – you may never get to taste my chocolate gingerbread cake.) I've been very affable to men – 'I've taken off my clothes . . .', etc. to quote. More to the point, I've been affable beyond the call of duty at readings. I have never complained when my hosts put me up in the red-light district, gave me dry toast only, didn't meet me when they'd promised or starved me throughout days of readings. I've behaved *like a fucking saint* on such occasions. If only we were asked somewhere together I could prove this to you.

Considering my only nastiness is against mean publishers, prejudiced judges (the Gregory Awards), etc., other poets ought to thank me for it. I'm doing it for all of us. Sadly, it seems they'd rather starve me out – my only cheques these days come from BBC radio or from TV. They're at least willing to pay me to perform; I don't know how I'd have survived the last few months otherwise. I'm going to try a last attempt at getting readings, etc. I'll write to the British Council offering my services and also place an ad. in the *LRB* offering to give readings or adjudicate:* it's a bit undignified but, who knows, it might get me past the literary mafia and through to those who dole out the cash. (End of whinge.)

I think I'll be affable after Easter. I have this problem – I swore to give up being nice to people for Lent.

˙ I've just had an all-female film crew in the house. In all my days as an extra I never saw a camerawoman before. This one was as nosy as a ferret – into all the darkest dirtiest rooms before I could stop her. She was pretending to look for a switch. As there were six in the crew I could not control where they went. The house still feels raped. My mother stayed below in a quiet state of panic. I've been filmed leaning out of the broken tower windows with my hair hanging down like Rapunzel – I couldn't understand why. It must be one of those arty films.

---

* The letter to the British Council got me nowhere. I have still, to date, done no readings for them. The advert in the *LRB* got me a few readings but I have never been asked to adjudicate a poetry competition.

The seagulls enjoyed it all. My pair – Hugo and Fifi – tried to get in on the act. Did I tell you I called the female Fifi? (Wishful thinking!) Sonny Jim has decamped to start his own life on another chimney, by the way.

What else is new? Shall I lambast anyone for you to help fill your column? I'm still in training at the local sports centre.

I hope you're better and that the marshmallow leaves helped. The tea made from the flowers tastes better, but they're very hard to find.

Love,
Fiona

14.4.88

Dear Hugo,
Thanks for your lovely letter. I'm very glad you're feeling better. I was worried you might have had to have some dreadful tests. Sympathy's no problem – you're never boring about yourself. You know I'm always happy to see you.

I've just read the *TLS* piece – sounds as if Hermine's book's still going through. I know the law: publishers are not entitled to break contracts just because their authors call them mean so-and-so's.

I shouldn't give up on the *TLS* pieces – you did them well. Maybe Israel will yield a tale. . . . Perhaps you could get away with less literature in the column? Perhaps it could be like *The Spectator*'s Low Life/High Life/Home Life ones; after all, it all comes under the heading of literature when a poet's writing it. I reckon you'd do Diary pieces well. I feel your anti-publisher column was a good brave piece, anyway. We should all be militant – it's our only chance of improving conditions.

Now, after the female film crew, it's torture by punk scaffolders. We are to have our tower done. We found the cheapest we could. They have a Down's syndrome boy to carry the bits, and most of the rest are punks who live in a squat. They have a common-law communal concubine, who's Chinese with crimson streaks in her mane. My neighbours have done nothing but complain. I think it's the punk bit that has been the last straw. Her-next-door is very bourgeois. 'I had to send my husband out to get the washing in when they started swearing.' She sweeps her path of lawn clippings with a dustpan and brush – and now the punks have buggered her mint.

I tell my mother that now our bourgeois cat has died we are shown up for what we are socially – owners of a ruin and a stinking tom cat. I wish I could fly to a seaside shack with you. I rather envy my beautiful gulls.

In the summer, come down for a hot lazy day – I promise not to fix you any lousy readings. We could eat strawberries from my garden if the scaffolders haven't killed them all, and swim in the sea, where I could show you my wonderful new muscles. Talking of muscles, I wonder if I might try weight-lifting. My hobby is experimenting on myself (hence the herbs and the henna). Weight-training made my legs sexier and gave me another half-inch in height last year. Perhaps I should try for another inch on the chest next? What do you think? Can't stand staying put.

Am I feeling the spring? In the spring a young woman's fancy lightly turns to thoughts of sex . . . just as it does in winter, autumn and summer in my case. Keep well, keep your pecker up (but only when you think of me). Love to come and see you when you're free. I might even feel like celebrating when/if I get another farthing (or some blood) out of Chatto.

> Love,
> Fiona

The following note was written on a postcard.

5.7.88

Hugo my dear,

The strawberries are in season (and extra large and juicy) *chez* Pitt-Kethley. . . . I have it in mind to make a chocolate ginger-bread cake also. If you want the Great British Seaside Day Out – winkles in the Old Town, fortune-telling machines, dirty post-cards, a sight of a stuffed albatross, a dip in the Channel, etc. – speak now or for ever hold your peace.

If you're too busy I shall give it all (and more) to my other men friends and you can bugger off, OK.

Love,
Fiona

PS Three days' notice required so I can muck out the ancestral pigsty.

Hugo's wife became ill, so he had a good excuse for refusing the seaside day out.

The following letter accompanied some poems Hugo had requested for a page of women's erotica that was planned for the *New Statesman*.

4.12.88

Dear Hugo,

Bet these are filthier than Cope's, Duffy's and Rowbotham's.

I'm enclosing (for a laugh) Dr Hugh's letter, or rather the transcript of it, ready-processed for the back of my next collection. That won't be out till November. Abacus wants some revolting fan letters to fill up the back of the book, so if you know anyone who writes revolting fan letters tell 'em to get in touch, for God's sake.

On the day I received the long-stemmed rose in a cellophane tube (about as romantic as a cock in a Durex or a furled umbrella) from the loony wanker of Oxford, I also was sent a cassette of *Les Misérables*. This came from a love-sick German banker. I had dropped him when I found out he had two wives and four children – a few too many even for me. Anyway, with the cassette came a version of one of the songs with funny little alterations – 'the hell I'm living' became 'the trap I'm living' in his rewrite. Very honest but very funny.

Things seem to be improving financially if not on other fronts. Maybe, just maybe, I will be able to afford a mortgage on something small down here come the next tax year. Property prices are dropping. It would make a pleasant change to have something to lure men to – a Gothic ruin with tom cat and Mother in residence hardly counts.

I have got photographeritis. Maybe they'd leave me alone if I ditched the marble halls. No end of people have done profiles and most have been spiked. It's all such a waste of time. I am sick of being exploited. The last sadist wanted me to strip off and dress up in a sheet. Having refused that, I didn't like to say no to lying on the marble stairs in a blue satin nightie. No wonder I'm fluey. If that Richard bloke gets in touch I shall certainly tell him to piss off. It's not all fun being a sex writer – I hardly get any time off to have sex.

I went to an odd dinner the other night; Tuppy Owens gave it as a prelude to the Sex Maniacs' Ball. I sat next to an American who said he'd been banished to Amsterdam for starting a magazine called *Suck*. On the other side was a pop star who'd had earrings or something inserted in his willy just for the hell of it. Anyway, I gobbled the fish soup and salmon very quickly, made my excuses and sprinted for the last train to Hastings before anyone took my name and address forcibly.

Love,
Fiona

My first name is Helen, I thought it might be a good joke to write a spoof letter under this name to Hugo's *alter ego* Sonny Jim, who's featured in many of his poems. I made Helen the sort of girl I thought Hugo/Sonny Jim might appreciate. I rather hoped Sonny Jim would correspond with Helen, but he didn't.

4.7.89

Dear Sonny Jim,

I hope you do not mind me writing to you out of the blue, but I couldn't resist. My older sister Fiona showed me some poems about you by Hugo Williams. (I think she's after him, so he'd better watch out.) I don't read much poetry – I'm not intellectual like her – but I felt very much moved and attracted towards you.

I expect you get a lot of these letters. Now, let me tell you a bit about myself. I am twice as gorgeous as Fiona and I never get in low papers like her. Unlike her I am a virgin (since the operation). I am not clever. My hobbies are travel, disco dancing, swimming in the sea and massage. I used to be a nurse . . . well, sort of – they let me wear a nurse's uniform where I was working, anyway. It was a sort of old men's hospital, I think – at least that's what they told me.

I think your Carnaby Street loons sound fab and groovy. Do you have a picture of yourself in them? If not, any other snapshot would do. I have a little heart-shaped frame that would be perfect for one of those passport photos or something smaller. I would love to know what you look like. I'm sure you look great.

At the moment I am living with Mother and Fiona. Fiona is trying to get us a cottage so that we can bring lots of men home without Mum complaining. She has her eye on one near the sea with a holly tree in front. It backs on to a mosque, which sounds noisy but is all right, because Hastings Borough Council doesn't allow them to have muezzins in a Neighbourhood Watch area.

Fiona is trying to beat the price down. It's not all that dear, but she's mean like that. She was going to buy a bigger Victorian house with rising damp in the Old Town. It was next to the Particular Baptists' chapel and opposite a hill with a path which leads to the nudist beach. She really fancied it but the building society didn't. I think the Particular Baptists told them not to lend her money on any property near them.

Bye for now. I do hope we can become pen pals.

Love,
Helen

At a party we went to later, Hugo gave several reasons for not having had an affair with me; he was too ordinary, he said, and I was too eccentric, 'a character'. This next letter was the last interesting one I wrote him. In it I pulled out every stop, arguing my case logically and trying to charm him at the same time. The reference to Grecian 2000 in the post-script was prompted by Hugo's daughter Murphy giving him some as a joke for Christmas. He gave it away, but then regretted not having tried it.

1.11.89

Dear Hugo,
You've got it all wrong. You are an extraordinary man and therefore you deserve an extraordinary woman. Here's a compliment that only an extraordinary woman would dare to pay. I'd rather win you than any millionaire or film star. Would you get that sort of adoration from an ordinary woman? I doubt it. Be warned, though – if I should decide to marry or live with someone I would be completely faithful to them and stop adoring you (let alone anything else). I believe in promiscuity before, not after, settling down. I have an inkling that you're a bit like Eugene Onegin. Do you know the story? You might deign

to fancy me as much as I fancy you when I have someone else and it's far too late. What was that you once said in some article about going in for 'impotence and loss'? What is it that men get by withholding sex from the women in their lives? Do they get chastity in that woman? Never. It is one of the prime facts of life that a woman who's denied sex with the man she craves finds pleasure elsewhere.

Now, you also think I'm dominant (like some of the ladies who advertise in the *Sunday Sport*?). Well, I'm submissive enough only to be dominant if chaps ask me to be. I much prefer them being on top or beside. Every time some toy-boy asks me to overpower him and get on top (the young ones like that), I think, 'Oh God, no, not again, this is too much effort!' I much prefer to be dominated sexually. It's a nice change from pretending to be superwoman and doing all the DIY. I've had a hard life, so I've had to be strong to survive. I had a weak but lovable father – always losing jobs. He died when I was twenty. I had to rush out as we had no phone and ring the ambulance because my mother didn't believe he was dead. I had to sort out his affairs because he'd left no will and everything was a complete mess. I had to rampage in the social-security office to get my mother's widow's pension and lend her money out of my student grant until it came. In the meantime my Welsh relatives descended and claimed I wasn't doing enough cooking and cleaning to help Mum. All I wanted was to sit and weep. I've had to be the man of the family since then, if not before. If that's made me strong and hard, do you wonder? Sex I loved because it was one area where I could be less hard, more myself, responsive, giving pleasure. If you think I'm dominant with men I fancy, you misunderstand me totally. In other ways I am only what I had to be to survive in hard conditions.

I prefer not to take the initiative sexually. The only time I ever made a pass was my ill-fated one at you. You'll just have to put my unfeminine action down to passion – it can mask the true personality in various ways. Now, I'm not really all that 'eccentric' or 'a character'. I was simply trying everything I could think of to dazzle/impress you. I fought hard for more money

mainly so that I could get somewhere less hellishly uncomfort-
able to invite you to. I was simply doing the Scheherazade
routine in a desperate attempt to please, or. . . . Every effort
I've made for you, hoping to please, gets misunderstood. I only
made the pass because I craved physical affection of some sort
from you. Was that dominant or eccentric? I doubt it.

Part 2: the newsy bit
   The new place is a bit like a Victorian doll's house. I got it
cheap – or cheap for the Old Town – because it was an execu-
tor's sale. Miss Ratcliff died (in her nineties) on your birthday
and the house had been empty since then, but it only went on
the market recently. I'm beginning to find out what Miss Ratcliff was like. Catalogues for the 'fuller figure' keep arriving,
which say on the front, 'Dear Miss Ratcliff, This is your lucky
day. We have drawn three lucky numbers which could win you
a birthday forecast and the chance of £25,000 when you order
from us.'
   I've just finished emulsioning the house from top to bottom
(in between articles). Bathrooms are just as good for watersports whatever colour they are, but I felt I had to change the
yellow. Then there was the gardenia wallpaper in the back
bedroom – five bloody coats to eradicate that (or was it six?).
Next comes the tiling in the bathroom. The Gas bastards took
three days to change the boiler and put in a shower. They'd
promised to do it in one, but what with cups of tea. . . . Too
little poetry is being written.
   I've also become more garden conscious. I felt I had to fertil-
ise the neglected front bit and wanted to do it for nothing. So, it
was up Barley Lane to follow the trail leading to the local hunter
trials. But I shan't tell you the rest of that tale in case you think
I'm eccentric. (Actually I'm just mean.) My back garden (garden
as in yard) is nice now – small but crammed with exotica. I
discovered camellias under the clematis and invested in a fan-
trained apple tree.
   I think I told you I've tested the nudist beach at Fairlight. You
have to be very fit to get there and even fitter to get back as it is

down a glen with huge steps cut in the cliffs. It's a lovely cove, though, and worth it. Two little boys (fully dressed) came to throw rocks at me while I was getting dried; then their father came up – ostensibly to restrain them. I was the only nude in the bloody place. The recent storms have put paid to my swimming a week or two early this year. I think my next dip will be in May. You must try it next summer – then at least there'd be two of us to brazen it out. Alternatively, if you can't manage the hike to Fairlight (or have something to hide from me) we can use other beaches.

I have some interesting new neighbours. The man next door has an aviary in his front room and also does embroidery. You really must see his front garden with its hand-painted notices about birds having no colour bar and its model of an old man on a seat. The man a house further down is a teddy boy (one of the original ones) and has a sheepdog called Elvis.

Ebenezer Road is very short – just a few houses – so it's very quiet. At the top there's a Regency chapel belonging to the Particular Baptists. If you go up the steps beside this and cross a quiet road you get into the country. It's all blackberries, nettles and naturists. There's a lot of really beautiful country quite near, I've only just realised, having never ventured that way before. Alternatively, the bottom corner of my road has a pub called The Stag. It has three dehydrated Elizabethan cats above the bar. They found them under the boards. A few houses up there's the church where Rossetti married. They're appealing for £150,000, but I'm not going to give them anything. I'm like that. The other direction leads down to the sea – five minutes' walk by OAP standards. I gun the pensioners down on my bike and do it in a minute. That's the end of the town where you can buy all the cheap fish. It has the fattest and most thuggish herring gulls you could wish to see. One of them lurks by a shellfish stall and pretends to limp when tourists pass. . . . That's by 'The Nellie' or The Nelson, where all the fishermen hang out hoping for a gale-force 9 so they can have another few pints. They tell the landlady interesting stories about deformed fish they've found and she believes them. Nearby is the Winkle

Club – an all-male centre for Freemason-like activities with winkles. Down on the beach there's my favourite museum; the prize exhibit's an albatross – a bit big for an Ancient Mariner's necklace. Coleridge was a bloody liar. Best remark heard in The Nelson: 'What's stuffing an albatross do to a bloke's luck?' (Comment by local artist.)

I've got some furniture but not enough to entertain in style yet. I shall be using the house more as a workplace for a while, so the phone number will work only till about 4 p.m. I'll go back and watch Ma's telly then if I haven't got anything else on. Most of the furniture's our old stuff, but I'm lashing out on a French antique bed. Should be good for my image, don't you think? I've hung up my nurse's uniform nearby. . . .

Here are the party details. Better bring the Abacus invitation. I'm sure they'll know me without it. I've mentioned your name to the *GQ* people so you should be able to get in without one there. I hope you can come to these. I'd love to see you – even if it is only as a friend for the moment. (Boo hoo!) It would be nice to have some fizz out of the literary world instead of the usual Tesco anti-freeze.

Love,
Fiona

PS If you really fancy some more Grecian 2000 (I think you're beautiful with or without it) then how does this idea grab you? Pluck up your courage. Go to the chemist's. If there's a bloke serving – fine. If it's a girl, spare your blushes and buy a packet of Durex instead.

The letters on the preceding pages are, in the main, presented uncut. I have taken out only a few postscripts that weren't interesting and a few unkind references to other people.

F.P-K.